GOOD WILL HUNTING

Good Will Hunting

SCREENPLAY

Matt Damon & Ben Affleck

WITH AN INTRODUCTION BY

Gus Van Sant

MIRAMAX
BOOKS

HYPERION
NEW YORK

Photos by George Kraychyk

Library of Congress Cataloging-in-Publication Data
Damon, Matt.
    Good Will Hunting : a screenplay / by Matt Damon and Ben Affleck ;
with an introduction by Gus Van Sant.–1st ed.
        p.   cm.
    ISBN 0-7868-8344-8 (alk. paper)
    I. Affleck, Ben, 1972– . II. Good Will Hunting (Motion picture)
III. Title.
PN1997.G62   1997
791.43'72—dc21
                                                                        97–44589
                                                                        CIP

Designed by Kathy Kikkert

First Edition

10   9   8   7   6

INTRODUCTION

It's obvious that these words come from a soulful place. Matt Damon and Ben Affleck are describing things in their screenplay that mean so much to each of them that it will break your heart when you read it. It is surprising that two boys their age (twenty-four and twenty-six) can speak so wisely about the human condition. They care so much about their lives, their friendships, and each other that I suppose all this humanity just pops out of them—somewhat like mathematical answers pop out of the shy mathematical genius character they have named Will. The creators have put together this story with such flawless clarity of purpose in their characters and with seemingly so little sweat that I consider them sort-of geniuses themselves for pulling it off.

It was three years ago when I was looking through the motion picture trade paper *Daily Variety* that the faces of Ben Affleck and Matt Damon caught my eye. They were smiling from an industry gossip column looking as if they had just won the lottery. *Good Will Hunting* was their first screenplay, which they had sold to a big company in Hollywood. There was apparently a lot of hoopla over the sale of this screenplay, and they were not even writers, they kept saying in the article—they were actors.

Not only did the press announcement cheerfully praise the prestigious and lucrative sale but also pointed out that it was very clever of Ben and Matt to have cast themselves in the lead parts—this was a secret plan of theirs, to be cast in parts that interested each of them, by writing the parts themselves.

The article went on, praising the buyers of the screenplay and the respective agents involved in putting the deal together; it was a great article about two young Hollywood actors, but it never dawned on me to try and ask for a copy of *Good Will Hunting* to read because the scripts in Hollywood were so hit or miss that I just didn't bother, never suspecting that it would contain any sort of genius. And it certainly didn't make me wonder whether or not one day I would be involved with the project or that I would ever meet up with the writers. Our first meeting would occur three years later.

It was in a Denny's on Sunset Boulevard that we met for the first time. A place where all three of us had spent a certain amount of downtime in our pasts. The usual cast of colorful characters surrounded us at nearby tables—out of work actors staring at cell phones which were propped up in front of them that they would gaze at longingly as if in conversation between sips of coffee.

"We're very proud of our friendship," Matt said.

"We've known each other since we were like seven," Ben added.

"We just arrived from New York."

"We drove across the country."

"How long did it take you?" I asked.

"Fifty-five . . . ?" Ben speculated.

"Fifty-seven hours," Matt said as a matter of fact.

"But the reason that we drive is we don't like to fly."

"Terrified of flying."

"We drive across the country about every two weeks."

"That's what it seems like."

Ben drives and Matt doesn't—even when they are staying in L.A., Ben often ends up driving Matt around like the character in *Good Will* named Chuckie who drives Will. (Note that at the end of the film *Good*

Will Hunting, Matt is driving the picture car and you can see how it's hard for him to steer a straight course.)

"When we say that we drove across the country, we mean that I drive and Matt rides along," Ben informs me.

"Fifty-five hours is fast, too," I say.

"Fifty-seven . . ."

"I mean . . ."

"Still fast though . . ."

"We're just trying to get to a meeting we have tomorrow at Fox and since we can't fly, we do this straight-through thing."

"Not a lot of sight-seeing." Matt says.

But Matt still doesn't take a turn at the wheel; he just makes up stories with Ben to keep him from falling asleep.

"A lot of *Good Will* was written on such cross-country road trips. We tell each other stories while in a particular character, usually to make each other laugh or to make sure that Ben doesn't fall asleep at the wheel."

"The stories have to be good or I start to nod off."

"So it sort of ups the ante as far as story quality goes. When we get into an improv that we both like, that we both think is going well and dialogue we are relatively excited by, I will open up the glove compartment where I keep my notebook and write down a few notes that we will use later to recall the entire improvisation," Matt says.

"When we do finally stop the car I'll unpack a laptop computer and we'll write down the new pages by reinventing it," Ben says.

"We also write by fax," Matt says.

"Fax?" I ask them.

"We were often apart because of acting commitments, so when I was filming in Alpine, Texas, and spending a lot of time indoors trying to get out of the the Texas heat I would write pages and send them off to Ben by fax. Ben was doing his film in Leadville, Colorado, and he would pick up the fax I sent to his production office, and work on the new pages and then send them back to me in Alpine."

"And let it be said," Ben adds, "that when we are doing this, most of the time we are trying to make ourselves laugh. We are going for a shared reaction. We're going for a good time."

"Or cry. We might make ourselves cry, too," Matt says.

"Yes, and also a lot of the time we'll have a few beers while we are writing. We're just hanging out with each other trying to entertain ourselves."

"When we happen to be staying in the same hotel we'll write on the weekends or on our days off. Part of the reason we worked on this script so much was that we often had huge amounts of time off in strange cities and there was absolutely no choice but to keep yourself occupied or go crazy from boredom, so we would write together to keep from going insane," Matt says.

I was witness to one of their many hotel room rewrites. There was a good deal of procrastination when during my particular visit. This could have been because they had been through so many rewrites before that they were tired of rewriting. There have been about ten rewrites in all. The first writing meeting that I had with them, we took a sight-seeing trip around West Memphis, Arkansas. Days later when things really got down to the wire and it seemed that we were just goofing off and hanging out and watching the hotel movies and really not getting anything done at all, that's when Ben and Matt would fly into action and create something almost spontaneously with Matt standing in the middle of the hotel room demonstratively gesturing and editing ideas by drawing dotted lines in the air with his hands, with Ben writing down dialogue on his laptop computer. Ben not only does the driving but he also does the typing.

Two best friends driving across deserts, faxing each other between remote locations, and hanging out in hotels trying to make each other laugh and cry over a three-year period is how they managed to put this amazing screenplay together.

There are no finely drawn heroes or villains in the script. There is no right or wrong particularly—there is something more like honor and dishonor within each character. In this screenplay it is okay to be wrong if you are honorable; the story is set in South Boston and this strikes me as a particularly South Boston viewpoint.

Good Will's central character, Will, is hiding from something—he doesn't know it but he is hiding his "good will" (which the character Sean hunts for), trading it to stay in a safe South Boston drinking establishment where he has a group of friends who protect him physically and emotionally. He has been hurt before and doesn't want to get hurt again by jeopardizing his safe surroundings and friends with change. Change has become for him a dire eventuality that he is doing his best to avoid as he grows closer to twenty-one years old.

"It is the story of a kid who doesn't want to get off his butt because it terrifies him," Matt says.

Will has extraordinary mathematical abilities which he keeps a secret. These abilities are something that all the other characters in the story either want a part of, or want to know more about, or want him to do something with. This story device is our Hitchcockian "maguffin"—the thing that all the characters in our story care desperately about but we as an audience don't particularly care about, at least not directly. What interests us as viewers is watching and listening to the characters discuss and fight over Will's good will.

The ideas of success, failure, and honor plague him while he struggles with whether it is safer to work an honest blue-collar job, which would allow him to continue to hide, or try for something more in line with the materialistic American dream. This supports *Good Will Hunting*'s pronounced academic class division.

In almost every scene, there is the construction or observation of an educational class structure. The young South Boston kids are the uneducated, poor, scrappy lower-class laborers with bleak prospects for a scholastic future, while the Cambridge teachers and students play in a privileged upper class. There is a particularly East Coast orientation to these distinctions of class and also an exaggeration between these differences. The lower class is the hero, the upper class the antihero. Although Will is emotionally uneducated, as a self-educated hero he is made out to be smarter than the most decorated MIT professor. It seems that education is suspect, but "smarts" are celebrated. Again, this strikes me as an Irish working-class drinking man's barside viewpoint, and is the emotional center for the storytellers.

Will's girlfriend, Skylar, is an English upper-class Harvard intellectual, producing a nice contrast to Will's Irish-American lower-class anti-intellectual.

In the center of the story is the character of Sean, a teacher who is rooted on both sides of this class system—an MIT–educated South Bostonian psychology professor who has chosen to teach at the working-class Bunker Hill Community College. Sean is a traditionally educated teacher for the people who also has "smarts," and he precipitates the well-constructed conflict in the story.

At first the screenplay seemed perhaps a little wordy. As Matt joked on the set when we shot the movie, the *Good Will* staging was usually two people sitting in chairs across from each other and talking. Only the backgrounds and the characters changed, and usually only one of the characters changed since Will is in virtually every scene. We wondered if this might become tiring, but as we forged ahead and began to shoot the film it became captivating, just as it was on the page.

The story of shooting the movie *Good Will Hunting* is a happy and somewhat uneventful one. It was made in Boston over the winter and spring of 1997. Robin Williams played Sean, Stellan Skarsgård played Lambeau, and Minnie Driver played Skylar. All three of these actors had a wonderful talent for bringing out the best of what we had to work with. At this writing, the movie has only been shown once to a preview audience, but if we can judge by that one screening it will have a great effect on Matt and Ben's careers.

—Gus Van Sant

GOOD WILL HUNTING

FADE IN:

■ **EXT. SOUTH BOSTON, ST. PATRICK'S DAY PARADE—DAY**

CUT TO:

■ **INT. L STREET BAR AND GRILLE, SOUTH BOSTON—EVENING**

The bar is dirty, more than a little run down. If there is ever a cook on duty, he's not here now. As we pan across several empty tables, we can almost smell the odor of last night's beer and crushed pretzels on the floor.

                            CHUCKIE
        Oh my God, I got the most fucked-up thing I been
        meanin' to tell you.

As the camera rises, we find FOUR YOUNG MEN seated around a table near the back of the bar.

                                ALL
        Oh, Jesus. Here we go.

The guy holding court is CHUCKIE SULLIVAN, twenty, and the largest of the bunch. He is loud, boisterous, a born entertainer. Next to him is WILL HUNTING, twenty, handsome and confident, a soft-spoken leader. On Will's right sits BILLY MCBRIDE, twenty-two, heavy, quiet, someone you defi-

nitely wouldn't want to tangle with. Finally there is MORGAN O'MALLY, nineteen, smaller than the other guys. Wiry and anxious, Morgan listens to Chuckie's horror stories with eager disgust.

All four boys speak with thick Boston accents. This is a rough, working-class Irish neighborhood, and these boys are its product.

> **CHUCKIE**
> You guys know my cousin Mikey Sullivan?

> **ALL**
> Yeah.

> **CHUCKIE**
> Well you know how he loves animals, right? Anyway, last week he's drivin' home . . .
> *(laughs)*

> **ALL**
> What? Come on!

> **CHUCKIE**
> *(trying not to laugh)*
> I'm sorry, 'cause you know Mikey, the fuckin' guy loves animals, and this is the last person you'd want this to happen to.

> **WILL**
> Chuckie, what the fuck happened?

> **CHUCKIE**
> Okay. He's drivin' along and this fuckin' cat jumps in front of his car, and so he hits this cat—

Chuckie is really laughing now.

> **MORGAN**
> —That isn't funny—

> **CHUCKIE**
> —and he's like, "Shit! Motherfucker!" And he looks in his rearview and sees this cat—I'm sorry—

2

BILLY

Fuckin' Chuckie!

CHUCKIE

So he sees this cat tryin' to make it across the street, and it's not lookin' so good.

WILL

It's walkin' pretty slow at this point.

MORGAN

You guys are fuckin' sick.

CHUCKIE

So Mikey's like, "Fuck, I gotta put this thing out of its misery." So he gets a hammer—

WILL/MORGAN/BILLY

OH!

CHUCKIE

—out of his tool box and starts chasin' the cat and starts whackin' it with the hammer. You know, tryin' to put the thing out of its misery.

MORGAN

Jesus.

CHUCKIE

And all the time he's apologizin' to the cat, goin' "I'm sorry." BANG! "I'm sorry." BANG!

BILLY

Like it can understand.

CHUCKIE

—And this Samoan guy comes runnin' out of his house and he's like, "What the fuck are you doing to my cat?!" Mikey's like, "I'm sorry"—BANG—"I hit your cat with my truck, and I'm just trying to put it out of its misery"—BANG! And the cat dies. So Mikey's like, "Why don't you come look at the front of my truck." 'Cause the other guy's all fuckin' flipped out about—

WILL

Watching his cat get brained.

Morgan gives Will a look, but Will only smiles.

CHUCKIE

Yeah, so he's like, "Check the front of my truck, I can prove I hit it 'cause there's probably some blood or something"—

WILL

—or a tail—

MORGAN

WILL!

CHUCKIE

And so they go around to the front of his truck . . . and there's another cat on the grille.

WILL/MORGAN/BILLY

No! Ugh!

CHUCKIE

Is that unbelievable? He brained an innocent cat!

BLACKOUT:

The opening credits roll over a series of shots of the city and the real people who live and work there, going about their daily lives.

■ EXT. SOUTH BOSTON—DAY

We see a panoramic view of South Boston.

■ INT. WILL'S APARTMENT—DAY

Will sits in his apartment, whose walls are completely bare. A bed, a small night table and an empty wastebasket adorn the room. A stack of twenty or so LIBRARY BOOKS sits by his bed. He is flipping through a book at about a page a second.

■ EXT. WILL'S APARTMENT—DAY

Chuckie stands on the porch to Will's house. His Oldsmobile idles by the curb. Will comes out and they get in the car.

■ EXT. M.I.T. CAMPUS, ESTABLISHING SHOT—DAY

We travel across crowded public housing and onto downtown. Finally, we gaze across the river and onto the great concrete-domed buildings that make up the M.I.T. campus.

CUT TO:

■ INT. M.I.T. CLASSROOM—DAY

The classroom is packed with graduate students and TOM, thirty-three, the professor's assistant. PROFESSOR LAMBEAU, fifty-two, is at the lectern. The chalkboard behind him is covered with theorems.

> LAMBEAU
> Please finish McKinley by next month. Many of you probably had this as undergraduates in real analysis. It won't hurt to brush up. I am also putting an advanced Fourier system on the main hallway chalkboard—

Everyone groans.

> LAMBEAU
> I'm hoping that one of you might prove it by the end of the semester. The first person to do so will not only be in my good graces, but go on to fame and fortune by having their accomplishment recorded and their name printed in the auspicious *M.I.T. Tech.*

Prof. Lambeau holds up a thin publication entitled M.I.T. Tech. Everyone laughs.

> LAMBEAU
> Former winners include Nobel Laureates, world-renowned astro-physicists, Field's Medal–winners, and lowly M.I.T. professors.

More laughs.

LAMBEAU

Okay. That is all.

A smattering of applause. Students pack their bags.

CUT TO:

■ **INT. FUNLAND—LATER**

The place is a monster indoor fun park. Will, Chuckie, Morgan and Billy are in adjoining batting cages. Will has disabled the pitching machine in his and pitches to Chuckie. The boys have been drinking. Will throws one to Chuckie, high and tight. Several empty beer cans sit by the cage.

CHUCKIE

Will!

Another pitch, inside.

CHUCKIE

You're gonna get charged!

WILL

You think I'm afraid of you, you big fuck? You're
crowdin' the plate.

Will guns another one, way inside.

CHUCKIE

Stop brushin' me back!

WILL

Stop crowdin' the plate!

Chuckie laughs and steps back.

CHUCKIE

Casey's bouncin' at a bar up Harvard. We should go up
there sometime.

WILL

What are we gonna do up there?

CHUCKIE

I don't know, we'll fuck up some smart kids.
(*stepping back in*)
You'd prob'ly fit right in.

WILL

Fuck you.

*Will fires a pitch at Chuckie's head. Chuckie dives to avoid being hit. He gets
up and whips his batting helmet at Will.*

CUT TO:

■ EXT. SOUTH BOSTON ROOFTOP—EARLY AFTERNOON

SEAN MAGUIRE, fifty-two, sits, FORMALLY DRESSED, on the roof of his apartment building in a beat-up lawn chair. Well built and fairly muscular, he stares blankly out over the city.

On his lap rests an open INVITATION that reads M.I.T. CLASS OF '72 REUNION.

While the morning is quiet, and Sean sits serenely, there is a look about him that tells us he has faced hard times. This is a man who has fought his way through life. On his lonely stare we:

CUT TO:

■ EXT. M.I.T. CAMPUS LAWN—DAY

A thirty-year REUNION PARTY has taken over the lawn. A well-dressed throng mills about underneath a large banner that reads: WELCOME BACK CLASS OF '72. We find Professor Lambeau standing with a drink in his hand, surveying the crowd. He is interrupted by an approaching STUDENT.

STUDENT

Excuse me, Professor Lambeau?

LAMBEAU

Yes.

STUDENT

I'm in your applied theories class. We're all down at the math and science building.

LAMBEAU

It's Saturday.

STUDENT

I know. We just couldn't wait till Monday to find out.

LAMBEAU

Find out what?

STUDENT

Who proved the theorem.

CUT TO:

■ **EXT. TOM FOLEY PARK, SOUTH BOSTON—AFTERNOON**

In the bleachers of the visiting section we find our boys, drinking and smoking cigarettes. Will pops open a beer. The boys have been here for a while and it shows.

Billy sees something that catches his interest.

BILLY

Who's that? She's got a nice ass.

Their P.O.V. reveals a girl in stretch pants talking to a beefy looking ITAL-IAN GUY (CARMINE SCARPAGLIA).

MORGAN

Yah, that is a nice ass.

CHUCKIE

You could put a pool in that backyard.

BILLY

Who's she talkin' to?

MORGAN

That fuckin' guinea, Will knows him.

WILL

Yah, Carmine Scarpaglia. He used to beat the shit outta me in kindergarten.

BILLY

He's a pretty big kid.

WILL

Yah, he's the same size now as he was in kindergarten.

MORGAN

Fuck this, let's get something to eat. . . .

CHUCKIE

What Morgan, you're not gonna go talk to her?

MORGAN

Fuck her.

The boys get up and walk down the bleachers.

WILL

I could go for a Whopper.

MORGAN
(nonchalant)

Let's hit Kelly's.

CHUCKIE

Morgan, I'm not goin' to Kelly's Roast Beef just 'cause you like the take-out girl. It's fifteen minutes out of our way.

MORGAN

What else we gonna do, we can't spare fifteen minutes?

CHUCKIE

All right Morgan, fine. I'll tell you why we're not goin' to Kelly's.

CHUCKIE

It's because the take-out bitch is a fuckin' idiot. I'm sorry you like her, but she's dumb as a post, and she has never got our order right, never once.

MORGAN

She's not stupid.

WILL

She's sharp as a marble.

CHUCKIE

We're not goin'.
                    (beat)
I don't even like Kelly's.

CUT TO:

■ INT. M.I.T. HALLWAY—LATER

Lambeau, still in his reunion formal wear, strides down the hallway, carrying some papers. A group of students has gathered by the chalkboard. They part like the Red Sea as he approaches the board. Using the papers in hand, he checks the proof. Satisfied, he turns to the class.

LAMBEAU

This is correct. Who did this?

Dead silence. Lambeau turns to an INDIAN STUDENT.

LAMBEAU

Nemesh?

Nemesh shakes his head in awe.

NEMESH

No way.

Lambeau erases the proof and starts putting up a new one.

LAMBEAU

Well, whoever you are, I'm sure you'll find this one
challenging enough to merit coming forward with your
identity. That is, if you can do it.

■ INT. CHUCKIE'S CAR, DRIVING IN SOUTH BOSTON—CONTINUOUS

*The street is crowded as our boys drive down Broadway. They move slowly
through heavy traffic, windows down. Chuckie sorts through a large KELLY'S
ROAST BEEF BAG as he drives.*

MORGAN

Double Burger.

Will holds the wheel for Chuckie as he looks through the bag.

MORGAN
(same tone)

Double Burger.

Chuckie gets out fries for himself, hands Will his fries.

MORGAN

I . . . I had a Double Burger.

CHUCKIE

Would you shut the fuck up! I know what you or-
dered, I was there!

MORGAN

So why don't you give me my sandwich?

CHUCKIE

What do you mean, *your* sandwich? I bought it.

MORGAN
(sarcastic)

Yah, all right . . .

CHUCKIE

How much money you got?

MORGAN

I told you, I just got change.

CHUCKIE

Well give me your fuckin' change and we'll put your
fuckin' sandwich on layaway.

MORGAN

Why you gotta be an asshole, Chuckie?

CHUCKIE

I think you should establish a good line of credit.

Laughter, Chuckie goes back to searching through the bag.

CHUCKIE

Oh motherfucker . . .

WILL

She didn't do it again, did she?

CHUCKIE

Jesus Christ. Not even close.

MORGAN

Did she get my Double Burger?

CHUCKIE

NO SHE DIDN'T GET YOUR DOUBLE BUR-
GER!! IT'S ALL FUCKIN' FLYIN' FISH FILLET!!

Chuckie whips a FISH SANDWICH back to Morgan, then another to Billy.

WILL

Jesus, that's really bad. Did anyone even order a Flyin'
Fish?

CHUCKIE

No, and we got four of 'em.

BILLY

You gotta be kiddin' me. Why do we even go to her?

CHUCKIE

'Cause fuckin' Morgan's got a crush on her, we always
go there, and when we get to the window he never
says a fuckin' word to her, he never even gets out of
the car, and she never gets our order right cause she's
the goddamn MISSING LINK!

WILL

Well, she outdid herself today. . . .

MORGAN

I don't got a crush on her.

Push in on Will, who sees something O.S.

*Will's P.O.V. reveals Carmine Scarpaglia and his friends walking down the
street. One of them casually lobs a bottle into a wire garbage can. It SHAT-
TERS and some of the glass hits a FEMALE PASSERBY who, although
unhurt, is upset.*

CHUCKIE

What do we got?

WILL

I don't know yet.

*WILL'S P.O.V.: The woman says something to Carmine. He says something
back. By the look on her face, it was something unpleasant.*

MORGAN

Come on, Will . . .

CHUCKIE

Shut up.

MORGAN

No, why didn't you fight him at the park if you
wanted to? I'm not goin' now, I'm eatin' my snack.

WILL

So don't go.

Will is out the door, jogging toward Carmine Scarpaglia. Billy gets out, following Will with a look of casual indifference.

> CHUCKIE
>
> Morgan, Let's go.

> MORGAN
>
> I'm serious, Chuckie. I ain't goin'.

Leaving the car, Chuckie opens his door to follow.

> CHUCKIE
> *(spins in his seat)*
> You're goin'. And if you're not out there in two
> fuckin' seconds, when I'm done with them you're next!

And with that, Chuckie is out the door.

CUT TO:

■ EXT. SIDEWALK—CONTINUOUS

Will comes jogging up toward Carmine Scarpaglia, calling out from across the street.

> WILL
> *(smiling, good-naturedly)*
> Hey, Carmine Scarpaglia! I went to kindergarten with
> you, right? Sister Margaret's class . . .

Carmine is bewildered by this strange interruption and unsure of Will's intentions. Just when it looks as though Carmine might remember him, Will DRILLS HIM with a sucker-punch, which begins the

■ FIGHT SEQUENCE: 40 FRAMES OVER M. GAYE'S "LET'S GET IT ON"

Will's momentum and respectable strength serve to knock the hapless Scarpaglia out cold. As soon as Will hits Carmine, Carmine's friends CONVERGE ON WILL. Billy JUMPS IN and wrestles one guy to the ground. The two exchange messy punches on the sidewalk.

Will is in trouble, back pedaling, dodging punches, trying to avoid being overrun. When he goes for one guy, another has an open shot and he HAMMERS

WILL with a right to the head. Will is staggering and bleary-eyed. As a second guy winds up for a shot, he is BLINDSIDED by Chuckie, who hits the kid as if he were a tackling sled, lifting him off the ground.

Chuckie turns to see Will still outnumbered. It's all Will can do to stay standing, as Morgan DROP-KICKS one of Scarpaglia's boys from the hood of a car. Contrary to what we might think, Morgan is quite a fighter. He peppers the kid with a flurry of blows.

The fight is messy, ugly and chaotic. Most punches are thrown wildly and miss; heads are banged against concrete; someone throws a bottle. In the end, it's our guys who are left standing, while Carmine's friends stagger off. Chuckie and Morgan turn to see Will, standing over the unconscious Carmine Scarpaglia, still POUNDING him.

■ ANGLE ON WILL: SAVAGE, UGLY, VICIOUS AND VIOLENT

Whatever demons must be raging inside Will, he is taking them out on Carmine Scarpaglia. He pummels the helpless, unconscious Scarpaglia, fury in his eyes. Chuckie and Billy pull Will away.

The POLICE finally arrive on the scene and having only witnessed Will's vicious attack on Scarpaglia, they grab him.

■ EXT. SIDEWALK (FULL SPEED)—CONTINUOUS

A crowd of onlookers has gathered. Chuckie addresses them.

> CHUCKIE
> Hey, thanks for comin' out.

> WILL
> Yeah, you're all invited over to Morgan's house for a complimentary fish sandwich.

The police slam Will onto the hood of a car.

> WILL
> (to police)
> Hey, I know it's not a French cruller, but it's free.

The cop holding Will SLAMS his face into the hood; another cop uses his baton to press Will's face into the car. The look of rage returns to Will's eye.

                                    WILL
        Get the fuck off me!

*Will resists. Another cop comes over. Will KICKS HIM IN THE KNEE,
dropping the cop. Momentarily freed, Will engages in a fracas with three cops.
More converge on Will, who—though he struggles—takes a beating.*

CUT TO:

■ **EXT. SEAN'S ROOF—DUSK**

*Sean sits exactly as we first saw him, except that his tie is now loose and an
empty bottle of IRISH WHISKY is at his side. He stares out over the city. A
MATRONLY LANDLADY comes out of a doorway on the roof.*

                                 LANDLADY
        Sean?

Sean doesn't answer.

                                 LANDLADY
        Sean? You okay? It's getting cold.

                                    SEAN
        Yeah.

                                 LANDLADY
                                  (beat)
        It's getting cold.

After a moment, she retreats back down the stairs. Sean doesn't move.

DISSOLVE:

■ **EXT. CHARLES RIVER, ESTABLISHING SHOT—MORNING**

The morning sun reflects brilliantly off the river.

CUT TO:

▪ EXT. COURTHOUSE—NEXT MORNING

Will emerges from the courthouse. Chuckie is waiting for him in the Cadillac with two cups of DUNKIN' DONUTS coffee. He hands one of them to Will. This feels routine.

> CHUCKIE
> When's the arraignment?

> WILL
> Next week.

Chuckie pulls away.

CUT TO:

▪ EXT. M.I.T. CAMPUS, ESTABLISHING SHOT—MORNING

Students walk to class, carrying bags. More than any other, students seem to be heading mostly into ONE PARTICULAR CLASSROOM.

▪ INT. M.I.T. CLASSROOM—MORNING

The classroom is even more crowded than when last we saw it. There is an atmosphere of excitement. Tom takes notes as Lambeau plays along, with mock pomposity and good humor.

> LAMBEAU
> Is it my imagination, or has my class grown considerably?

Laughter.

> LAMBEAU
> I look around and see young people who are my students, young people who are not my students, as well as some of my colleagues. And by no stretch of my imagination do I think you've all come to hear me lecture—

More laughter.

LAMBEAU

—but rather to ascertain the identity of who our esteemed *Tech* has come to call "The Mystery Math Magician."

He holds up the M.I.T. *Tech, which features a silhouetted figure emblazoned
with a large, white question mark. The headline reads MYSTERY MATH MAGI-
CIAN STRIKES AGAIN*

LAMBEAU

Whoever you are, you've solved four of the most difficult theorems I've ever given a class. So without further
ado, come forward silent rogue, and receive thy prize.

*The class waits in breathless anticipation. A STUDENT shifts his weight in his
chair, making a noise.*

LAMBEAU

Well, I'm sorry to disappoint my spectators, but it appears there will be no unmasking here today. I'm going
to have to ask those of you not enrolled in the class to
make your escape now, or for the next three hours be
subjected to the mundanity of eigenvectors.

*People start to gather their things and go. Lambeau picks up a piece of chalk and
starts writing on the board.*

LAMBEAU

However, my colleagues and I have conferred. There is
a problem on the board, right now, that took us two
years to prove. So let this be said; the gauntlet has been
thrown down. But the faculty have answered the chal-
lenge, and answered with vigor.

CUT TO:

■ INT. M.I.T. HALLWAY—NIGHT

*Lambeau comes out of his office with Tom and locks the door. As he turns to
walk down the hallway, he stops. A faint TICKING SOUND can be heard.
He turns and walks down the hall.*

*Lambeau and Tom come around a corner. Their P.O.V. reveals a figure in sil-
houette blazing through the proof on the chalkboard. There is a mop and bucket
beside him. As Lambeau draws closer, reveal that the figure is Will, in his janitor's uniform. There is a look of intense concentration in his eyes.*

LAMBEAU

Excuse me!

Will looks up, immediately starts to shuffle off.

WILL

Oh, I'm sorry.

LAMBEAU

What are you doing?

WILL
(walking away)

I'm sorry.

Lambeau follows Will down the hall.

LAMBEAU

What's your name?
                    (beat)
Don't you walk away from me. This is people's work,
you can't graffiti here.

WILL

Hey, fuck you.

LAMBEAU
(flustered)
Well . . . I'll be speaking to your supervisor.

Will walks out. Lambeau goes to "fix" the proof, scanning the blackboard for whatever damage Will caused. He stops, scans the board again. Amazement registers on his face.

LAMBEAU

My God.

Down the hall, we hear the DOOR CLOSE. He turns to look for Will, who is gone.

CUT TO:

■ **EXT. BOW AND ARROW PUB, CAMBRIDGE—THAT NIGHT**

A crowded Harvard Bar. Will and our gang walk by a line of several Harvard students, waiting to be carded.

MORGAN

What happened?
                    (beat)
You got fired, huh?

WILL

Yeah, Morgan. I got fired.

MORGAN
(starts laughing)
How fuckin' retarded do you have to be to get shit–
canned from that job? How hard is it to push a fuckin'
broom?

CHUCKIE

You got fired from pushin' a broom, you little bitch.

MORGAN

Yah, that was different. Management was restructurin'—

BILLY

—Yah, restructurin' the number of retards they had
workin' for them.

MORGAN

Fuck you, you fat fuck.

BILLY

Least I work for a livin'.
(to Will)
Why'd you get fired?

WILL

Management was restructurin'.

Laughter.

CHUCKIE

My uncle can probably get you on my demo team.

MORGAN

What the fuck? I just asked you for a job yesterday!

CHUCKIE

I told you no yesterday!

After two students flash their IDs to the doorman (CASEY) our boys file past
him.

ALL
(one after another)
What's up, Case?

With an imperceptible nod, Casey waves our boys through. A fifth kid, a
HARVARD STUDENT, tries to follow. He is stopped by Casey's massive
outstretched arm:

I.D.?

■ INT. BOW AND ARROW—CONTINUOUS

Chuckie is collecting money from the guys to buy a pitcher. All but Morgan cough up some crumpled dollars.

CHUCKIE

So this is a Harvard bar, huh? I thought there'd be equations and shit on the wall.

■ INT. BACK SECTION, BOW AND ARROW—MOMENTS LATER

Chuckie returns to a table where Will, Morgan and Billy have made themselves comfortable. He spots two ATTRACTIVE YOUNG HARVARD WOMEN sitting together at the end of the bar. Chuckie struts his way toward the women and pulls up a stool. He flashes a smile and tries to submerge his thick Boston accent.

CHUCKIE

Hey, how's it goin'?

LYDIA

Fine.

SKYLAR

Okay.

CHUCKIE

So, you ladies, ah, go to school here?

LYDIA

Yes.

CHUCKIE

Yeah, 'cause I think I had a class with you.

At this point, several interested parties materialize. Morgan, Billy and Will try, as inconspicuously as possible, to situate themselves within listening distance. A rather large student in a HARVARD LACROSSE sweatshirt, CLARK, twenty-two, notices Chuckie. He walks over to Skylar and Lydia, nobly hovering over them as protector. This gets Will, Morgan and Billy's attention.

SKYLAR
What class?

CHUCKIE
Ah, history I think.

SKYLAR
Oh . . .

CHUCKIE
Yah, it's not a bad school . . .

At this point, Clark can't resist and steps in.

CLARK
What class did you say that was?

CHUCKIE
History.

CLARK
How'd you like that course?

CHUCKIE
Good, it was all right.

CLARK
History? Just "history"? It must have been a survey
course, then.

*Chuckie nods. Clark notices Chuckie's clothes. Will and Billy exchange a look
and move subtly closer.*

CLARK
Pretty broad. History of the world?

CHUCKIE
Hey, come on pal, we're in classes all day.
(beat)
That's one thing about Harvard never seizes to amaze
me, everybody's talkin' about school all the time.

CLARK

Hey, I'm the last guy to want to talk about school at
the bar. But as long as you're here I want to "seize" the
opportunity to ask you a question.

*Billy shifts his beer into his left hand. Will and Morgan see this. Morgan rolls
his eyes as if to say, "Not again . . ."*

CLARK

Oh, I'm sure you covered it in your history class.

*Clark looks to see if the girls are impressed. They are not. When Clark looks
back to Chuckie, Skylar turns to Lydia and rolls her eyes. They laugh. Will
sees this and smiles.*

CHUCKIE

To tell you the truth, I wasn't there much. The class
was rather elementary.

CLARK

Elementary? Oh, I don't doubt that it was. I remember
the class—it was just between recess and lunch.

Will and Billy come forward, stand behind Chuckie.

CHUCKIE

All right, are we gonna have a problem?

CLARK

There's no problem. I was just hoping you could give
me some insight into the evolution of the market econ-
omy in the early colonies. My contention is that prior
to the Revolutionary War, the economic modalities,
especially of the southern colonies, could most aptly be
characterized as agrarian precapitalist and . . .

*Will, who at this point has migrated to Chuckie's side and is completely fed up,
includes himself in the conversation.*

WILL

Of course that's your contention. You're a first-year
grad student.

You just finished reading some Marxian historian, Pete Garrison prob'ly, and so naturally that's what you believe until next month when you get to James Lemon and get convinced that Virginia and Pennsylvania were strongly entrepreneurial and capitalist back in seventeen forty. That'll last until sometime in your second year, then you'll be in here regurgitating Gordon Wood about the prerevolutionary utopia and the capital-forming effects of military mobilization.

CLARK
(taken aback)
Well, as a matter of fact, I won't, because Wood drastically underestimates the impact of—

WILL
—Wood drastically underestimates the impact of social distinctions predicated upon wealth, especially inherited wealth. . . . You got that from Vickers's *Work in Essex County*, was it pages ninety-eight to one-oh-two, what? Do you have any thoughts of your own on the subject or were you just gonna plagiarize the whole book for me?

Clark is stunned.

WILL
Look, don't try to pass yourself off as some kind of an intellect at the expense of my friend just to impress these girls.

Clark is lost now, searching for a graceful exit, any exit.

WILL
The sad thing is, in about fifty years you might start doin' some thinkin' on your own and by then you'll realize there are only two certainties in life.

CLARK
Yeah? What're those?

WILL

One, don't do that. Two, you dropped a hundred and
fifty grand on an education you coulda picked up for a
dollar fifty in late charges at the public library.

Will catches Skylar's eye.

CLARK

But I will have a degree, and you'll be serving my kids
fries at a drive-through on our way to a skiing trip.

WILL
(smiles)
Maybe. But at least I won't be unoriginal.
(beat)
And if you got a problem with that, I guess we can step
outside and deal with it that way.

*While Will is substantially smaller him, Clark decides not to take Will up on
his offer.*

WILL

If you change your mind, I'll be over by the bar.

*He turns and walks away. Chuckie follows, throwing Clark a look. Morgan
turns to a nearby girl.*

MORGAN

My boy's wicked smart.

■ **INT. BOW AND ARROW, AT THE BAR—LATER**

*Will sits with Morgan at the bar, watching with some amusement as Chuckie
and Billy play a bar basketball game where the players shoot miniature balls at a
small basket. In the background we occasionally hear Chuckie shouting,
"Larry!" when he scores. Skylar emerges from the crowd and approaches Will.*

SKYLAR

You suck.

                    WILL

What?

                    SKYLAR

I've been sitting over there for forty-five minutes waiting for you to come talk to me. But I'm just tired now
and I have to go home, and I wasn't going to keep sitting there waiting for you.

                    WILL

I'm Will.

                    SKYLAR

Skylar. And by the way, that guy over there is a real
dick, and I just wanted you to know he didn't come
with us.

                    WILL

I kind of got that impression.

                    SKYLAR

Well, look, I have to go. Gotta get up early and waste
some more money on my overpriced education.

                    WILL

I didn't mean you. Listen, maybe . . .

                    SKYLAR

Here's my number.

Skylar produces a folded piece of paper and offers it to Will.

                    SKYLAR

Maybe we could go out for coffee sometime?

                    WILL

Great, or maybe we could go somewhere and just eat a
bunch of caramels.

                    SKYLAR

What?

                              WILL

When you think about it, it's just as arbitrary as drinking coffee.

                             SKYLAR
                             (laughs)

Okay, sounds good.

She turns.

                              WILL

Five minutes.

                             SKYLAR

What?

                              WILL

I was tryin' to be smooth.
                        (indicates clock)
But at twelve-fifteen I was gonna come over there and
talk to you.

                             SKYLAR

See, it's my life story. Five more minutes and I would
have got to hear your best pick-up line.

                              WILL

The caramel thing is my pick-up line.

                             SKYLAR
                             (beat)

Glad I came over.

CUT TO:

■ EXT. BOW AND ARROW—LATER

*Our boys are walking out of the bar, teasing one another about their bar-ball
exploits. Across the street is another bar with a glass front. Morgan spots Clark
sitting in the window with some friends.*

                    MORGAN
There's that fuckin' Barney right now, with his fuckin'
"skiin' trip." We shoulda kicked that dude's ass.

                    WILL
Hold up.

*Will crosses the street, approaches the plate glass window and stands across from
Clark, separated only by the glass. He POUNDS THE GLASS to get
Clark's attention.*

                    WILL
Hey!

Clark turns toward Will.

                    WILL
DO YOU LIKE APPLES?

Clark doesn't get it.

                    WILL
DO YOU LIKE APPLES?!

                    CLARK
Yeah?

Will SLAMS SKYLAR'S PHONE NUMBER against the glass.

                    WILL
WELL I GOT HER NUMBER! HOW DO YA
LIKE THEM APPLES?!!

Will's boys erupt into laughter. Angle on Clark, deflated.

■ **EXT. STREET—NIGHT**

The boys make their way home, piled in Chuckie's car, laughing together.

■ **EXT. CHARLES STREET BRIDGE—DAWN**

Shot of car crossing over the Charles St. Bridge, overtaking a Red-line train.

■ **EXT. CHARLESTOWN BACK ROAD—DAWN**

Traveling through narrow back roads in Charlestown, passing the Bunker Hill monument.

■ **EXT. WILL'S APARTMENT—DAY**

Arriving at Will's house and dropping him off.

DISSOLVE TO:

■ **INT. M.I.T. BUILDINGS AND GROUNDS GARAGE—DAY**

Lambeau walks into a small garage facility. The area stores lawn machinery and various tools. An older man, TERRY, fifty-eight, sits behind the desk reading the BOSTON HERALD sports page. Lambeau has obviously never been here before. He takes in the surroundings, somewhat uncomfortably. Gets dirty.

LAMBEAU

Excuse me. Is this the buildings and grounds office?

TERRY

Yeah, can I help you?

                    LAMBEAU
I'm trying to find the name of a student who works
here.

                    TERRY
No students work for me.

                    LAMBEAU
Could you just check, because the young man who
works in my building—

                    TERRY
Which one's your building?

                    LAMBEAU
Building Two.

Terry checks a list behind his desk. Looks up.

                    TERRY
Well, if something was stolen, I should know about it.

                    LAMBEAU
No, no. Nothing like that. I just need his name.

                    TERRY
I can't give you his name unless you have a complaint.

                    LAMBEAU
Please, I'm a professor here and it's very important.

                    TERRY
Well, he didn't show up for work today . . .

Terry takes a beat. Holding all the cards.

                    TERRY
Look, he got this job through his P.O., so you can call
him.

*Terry goes through a stack of papers on his desk. He takes out a card and hands
it to Lambeau. Lambeau looks blankly at the card, which reads: PAROLE EM-
PLOYMENT PROGRAM.*

Will stands before JUDGE MALONE, forty, for arraignment. It is fairly un-
ceremonious. The courtroom is nearly empty, save for Will and the PROSE-
CUTOR. Lambeau walks in from the back.

> **WILL**
> There is a lengthy legal precedent, Your Honor, going
> back to seventeen eighty-nine, whereby a defendant
> may claim self-defense against an agent of the govern-
> ment, where the act is shown to be a defense against
> tyranny, a defense of liberty—

The judge interrupts to address the prosecutor.

> **JUDGE MALONE**
> Mr. Simmons, Officer McNeely, who signed the com-
> plaint, isn't in my courtroom. Why is that?

> **PROSECUTOR**
> He's in the hospital with a broken knee, Your Honor.
> But I have depositions from the other officers.

> **WILL**
> Henry Ward Beecher proclaimed in his *Proverbs from*
> *Plymouth Pulpit* back in eighteen eighty-seven, that
> "Every American citizen is, by birth, a sworn officer of
> the state. Every man is a policeman." As for the other
> officers, even William Congreve said, "he that first cries
> out 'stop thief' is oft he that has stolen the treasure."

> **PROSECUTOR**
> Your Honor—

Will cranks it up.

> **WILL**
> *(to Prosecutor)*
> I am afforded the right to speak in my own defense by
> our Constitution, sir. The same document which guar-
> antees my right to liberty. "Liberty," in case you've
> forgotten, is "the soul's right to breathe, and when it

cannot take a long breath laws are girded too tight. Without liberty, man is in syncope."
> *(beat, to judge)*

Ibid. Your Honor.

PROSECUTOR

Man is a what?

WILL

Julius Caesar proclaimed—though he be wounded— "Magna . . ."

The Judge interrupts.

JUDGE MALONE

Son,

> *(beat)*

my turn.

The judge opens Will's CASE HISTORY.

JUDGE MALONE
> *(reading)*

June 'ninety-three, assault, September 'ninety-three assault . . . Grand theft auto February 'ninety-four . . .

A beat, the judge takes particular notice.

JUDGE MALONE

. . . where apparently you defended yourself and had the case thrown out by citing "free property rights of horse and carriage" from seventeen ninety-eight . . .

Lambeau has to smile, impressed. The judge shakes his head.

JUDGE MALONE

March 'ninety-four, public drunkenness, public nudity, assault. October ninety-four, mayhem. November 'ninety-four, assault. January 'ninety-five, impersonating a police officer, mayhem, theft, resisting—overturned—

The judge takes a beat. Gives Will a look.

JUDGE MALONE

You're in my courtroom now, and I am aware of your
priors.
(beat)
I'm also aware that you're an orphan. You've been
through several foster homes. The state removed you
from three because of serious physical abuse.

The judge holds a look on Will, who looks down.

JUDGE MALONE

Another judge might care. You hit a cop, you go in.
(beat)
Motion to dismiss denied.

The bailiff comes forward to remove Will from the courtroom.

JUDGE MALONE

Keep workin' on your arguments, son. A word of advice for trial: Speak English.

*As Will is removed from the courtroom, Lambeau approaches Judge Malone,
who is stepping down from the bench.*

LAMBEAU

Excuse me, Your Honor.
(offers hand)
Gerald Lambeau.

An awkward beat. Lambeau waits for some sign of recognition.

LAMBEAU

I'm a professor at M.I.T.
(beat)
Combinatorial mathematics.

The judge offers only a blank look.

JUDGE MALONE

Oh. Pleased to meet you.

LAMBEAU

Do you have a minute?

CUT TO:

■ INT. MIDDLESEX COUNTY JAIL, HOLDING AREA—SAME

A GUARD walks Will down a hallway toward a group of phones.

> **GUARD**
> One call, to an attorney.
> *(beat)*
> One.

The guard gives Will a hard look for a beat. Then leaves.

> **WILL**
> How many?

Will picks up the phone, dials.

> **WILL**
> Hey, Skylar?

■ INT. SKYLAR'S DORM—DAY

> **SKYLAR**
> Yeah?

> **WILL**
> It's Will, the really funny good-looking guy you met at the bar?

> **SKYLAR**
> I'm sorry, I don't recall meeting anyone who fits that description.

> **WILL**
> Okay, you got me. It's the ugly, obnoxious, toothless loser who got drunk and wouldn't leave you alone all night.

> **SKYLAR**
> Oh Will! I was wondering when you'd call.

WILL
Yeah, I figured maybe sometime this week we could go to a café and have some caramels.

SKYLAR
Sounds good, where are you now?

WILL
You aren't, by any chance, pre-law, are you?

CUT TO:

■ **INT. MIDDLESEX COUNTY JAIL, INTERROGATION ROOM—LATER**

Professor Lambeau sits, waiting. Will is brought in, shackled, by the guard.

LAMBEAU

Hello. Gerald Lambeau, M.I.T.

WILL

Fuck do you want?

LAMBEAU

I've spoken with the judge and he's agreed to release
you under my supervision.

WILL
(suspicious)

Really?

LAMBEAU

Yes. Under two conditions.

WILL

What're those?

LAMBEAU

That you meet with me twice a week—

WILL

What for?

LAMBEAU

Go over the proof you were working on, get into some
more advanced combinatorial mathematics, finite math—

WILL

Sounds like a real hoot.

LAMBEAU

The other condition is that you see a therapist.

WILL

Oh, come on.

LAMBEAU

The judge was very clear about this: You're to meet
with me and a therapist twice a week and I'm responsi-

ble to submit reports on these meetings. If you fail to
meet any of these conditions, the judge told me you
will have to serve time.

                    WILL
If I agree to this, I walk right now?

                  LAMBEAU
That's right.

                    WILL
I'll do the work. I'm not gonna meet with a therapist.

                  LAMBEAU
Now, it won't be as bad as it sounds, Will.
                   (beat)
I've already spoken to one therapist, his name is Henry
Lipkin and he's a friend of mine. He's also published
four books and is widely considered to be one of the
brightest men in his field.
                   (beat)
I'm sure it'll be better than jail.

CUT TO:

■ **INT. FUNLAND—DAY**

*Will and Chuckie walk up to an enclosed trampoline. Billy and Morgan prefer
to use it for their own version of "Wrestlemania." As Will and Chuckie ap-
proach, Billy is on top of a bloodied Morgan and has him in the "cobra clutch."
Will and Chuckie watch for a beat. Billy tightens his grip.*

                   BILLY
Submit, bitch! Submit! Submit!

                  MORGAN
            (being strangled)
Suck my cock.

                   BILLY
Oh, Morgan!

Chuckie turns to Will conspiratorially, as they wait for the fight to finish.

CHUCKIE
What'd you get? You get leniency?

WILL
Probation, counselin', few days a week.

CHUCKIE
You're fuckin' good.

Will smiles.

CHUCKIE
Just submit, Morgan. He's got you in the cobra clutch.

MORGAN
(to Chuckie)
Fuck your mother, too!

■ **INT. WILL'S APARTMENT—NIGHT**

Will sits alone in his one-room apartment, reading. A closer look reveals he is reading a self-help PSYCHOLOGY BOOK. Will is flipping through the book at about a page a second. He shakes his head and smiles. Upon finishing the book, he throws it in a nearby WASTEBASKET. Push in on the back of the book where a SMILING PSYCHOLOGIST is pictured.

■ **INT. PSYCHOLOGIST'S OFFICE—CONTINUOUS**

Will sits in a well-decorated psychologist's office. Across from Will sits the PSY-CHOLOGIST, HENRY LIPKIN, forty, from the book. They are in mid-session.

WILL
That's why I love stock-car racin'. That Dale Ernhart's real good.

PSYCHOLOGIST
Now you know, Will, and I know, what you need to be doing. You have a gift.

WILL
I could work the pit maybe, but I could never drive like Dale Ernhart—

PSYCHOLOGIST

—You have a quality—something you were born with, that you have no control over—and you are, in a sense, hiding that by becoming a janitor. And I'm not saying that's wrong. I'm friends with the janitor that works in my building. He's been to my house for dinner. As a matter of fact, I did some free consultation for "Mike"— that's not his real name. That's in my book.

WILL

Yeah, I read your book. "Mike" had the same problems as "Chad" the stockbroker.

PSYCHOLOGIST

Yes. The pressures you feel, and again, I am neither labeling nor judging them, are keeping you from fulfilling your potential—you're in a rut. So stop the tomfoolery, the shenanigans, Will.

WILL

You're right. I know.

PSYCHOLOGIST

Will, you're not getting off that easy.

WILL

No, but, I mean you know . . . I do other things. That no one knows about.

PSYCHOLOGIST

Like what, Will?

WILL

I go places, I interact.

PSYCHOLOGIST

What places?

WILL

Certain clubs.
                    (beat)
Like, the Fantasy. It's not bad.

Will gives the psychologist a furtive look.

WILL

It's just that feeling when you can take your shirt off
and really dance.
                    (beat)
When the music owns you. Do you understand?

PSYCHOLOGIST

I might understand that.

WILL

Do you find it hard to hide the fact that you're gay?

PSYCHOLOGIST

What?

WILL

C'mon, I read your book. I talked to you. It's just something I know to be true.

PSYCHOLOGIST

That's very presumptuous.

WILL

Buddy, two seconds ago you were ready to give me a
jump.

PSYCHOLOGIST
                    (a little laugh)
Well, I'm sorry to disappoint you, but I'm married and
I have two children.

WILL

I'm sure you do. You probably got a real nice house,
nice car—your book's a best-seller.

                    PSYCHOLOGIST
You're getting defensive, Will.

                        WILL
Look, man. I don't care if you're putting from the
rough. There are solid arguments that some of the
greatest people in history were gay: Alexander the
Great, Caesar, Shakespeare, Oscar Wilde, Napoleon,
Gertrude Stein, not to mention Deney Terrio—not
many straight men can dance like that.

                    PSYCHOLOGIST
Who is Deney Terrio?

                        WILL
If you wanna hit Ramrod, take your shot. Take some
pride in it. You go to church? So fuckin' what? God
loves you. I mean, Christ, a guy as well known as you?
By the time you put your disguise on and skulk out of
the house Sunday nights you prob'ly look like Inspector
Clouseau.

The psychologist calmly packs his things.

                    PSYCHOLOGIST
Well, I can see this is pointless . . .

                        WILL
You're getting defensive . . . Henry. And hey, Chief—
tell the wife, at least. Christ, set her free. She's probably
been dying for it.

The shrink gets up and walks out.

                        WILL
Fuckin' hypocrite . . .

■ INT. HALLWAY—CONTINUOUS

*The psychologist comes walking out, much to the surprise of Lambeau and Tom,
who have been waiting in the lobby.*

LAMBEAU
Henry?

The psychologist keeps walking.

PSYCHOLOGIST
No. You know what, Gerry? This is why I don't do
pro bono anymore. It's not worth it to me.

LAMBEAU
What happened?

PSYCHOLOGIST
I don't have the time. I'm going on national televison
this week.

LAMBEAU
Wait a minute, Henry . . .

He is out the door. Lambeau looks to Tom.

CUT TO:

■ **INT. LAMBEAU'S OFFICE—DAY**

*Will is in Lambeau's office. Lambeau is at the board, working on a diagram as
Tom takes notes. Will seems disinterested.*

LAMBEAU
This rectangle is subdivided into rectangles. One edge
of an inner rectangle is an integer. Can you prove that
one edge of the larger rectangle is an integer?

WILL
Of course.

LAMBEAU
Okay. How?

WILL
It's an integer proof.

Lambeau smiles.

WILL

What? Hey look, buddy, my time's almost up. You
want me to sit here for an hour and write it out?

Lambeau says nothing. Will gets up and goes to the board.

WILL

Look, I'll give you the key steps to it but I'm not
gonna do the whole thing.

Lambeau keeps smiling.

LAMBEAU

That would be a monumental waste of time, wouldn't
it, Will?

WILL

I think so.

LAMBEAU

I happen to know so.

Lambeau rises and goes to the board.

LAMBEAU

You're thinking too hard. What if I did this?

He draws a vertical line through the diagram.

LAMBEAU

Now, what if I do this?

He draws a horizontal line through the diagram. He hands Will the chalk.

LAMBEAU

Have you ever played checkers?

*Will realizes what Lambeau is getting at. In a flash he starts drawing lines
through the diagram, energized.*

                              WILL

You color-code it. Half red, half black. If that's an integer—

Lambeau steps in, writing with him.

                            LAMBEAU

What's that?

                              WILL

Half red, half black—

                            LAMBEAU

—That?—

                              WILL

—Half red, half black—

                            LAMBEAU

That edge!

                              WILL

An integer.

*The two stop. They are silent for a moment. Like two gunfighters after a duel,
they put down the chalk.*

                            LAMBEAU
                        (checks his watch)
It would appear we got that proof in under the wire after all. It's not how hard you look at things, young man;
it's the way you look at them. If you take aim before
you fire, you will find the most difficult problems become, quite literally, child's play.

Will gets his coat.

                            LAMBEAU

Will, you've managed to offend four of my colleagues
so much that they refused to come back. You're meeting with the leading hypnotist in the country next
week and Tom and I plan to sit in on the sessions, so I
expect you to behave appropriately.

CUT TO:

■ INT. LAMBEAU'S OFFICE—DAY

Will sits in a chair across from Lambeau and the HYPNOTIST. Tom takes notes. The hypnotist makes small talk with Lambeau, who checks his watch.

> **LAMBEAU**
> Shall we start the, uh . . .

> **WILL**
> Yeah, when do I get my hypnosis? You guys been talkin' for twenty minutes.

> **HYPNOTIST**
> Yes, Will. We'll get to that. But first, why don't you go to sleep for me.

He SNAPS HIS FINGERS and instantly Will's head goes BACK and his EYES CLOSE. The hypnotist gives Lambeau a look.

> **HYPNOTIST**
> Would you mind standing on one leg?

Will gets up and stands on one leg. Lambeau is impressed.

TIME CUT TO:

■ INT. LAMBEAU'S OFFICE—LATER

Will is reclining, eyes closed, in a trancelike state. The mood is more serious now.

> **HYPNOTIST**
> Okay, you're in your bed, Will. Now, how old are you?

> **WILL**
> Seven.

HYPNOTIST
And what do you see?

WILL
Somethin's in my room.

HYPNOTIST
What is it?

WILL
It's like a small figure, hoverin' over me. Gettin' closer.

Will flinches.

HYPNOTIST
You're in a safe place, Will.

WILL
It's touching me.

Lambeau makes a sound. The hypnotist shushes him with his finger. Tom returns to his note taking.

HYPNOTIST
Where is it touching you?

WILL
Down there.
                    (indicating genitals)
And I'm nervous.

HYPNOTIST
You don't have to be nervous, Will.

Lambeau and the therapist trade looks. This is working.

WILL
—'cause I'm not ready.
                    (calming)

48

But the figure tells me everything's gonna be all right. 'Cause the figure's a Libra, too. And we start dancin' and it's beautiful—

Will breaks into song at full volume.

WILL
SKY ROCKETS IN FLIGHT!

LAMBEAU
(getting up)
Oh, Jesus.

The hypnotist gets up and starts heading toward the door. Will is still singing from "Sky Rockets."

LAMBEAU
Wait a minute, Barry.

HYPNOTIST
I have better ways to spend my time.

He is gone. Will stops singing, laughs.

LAMBEAU
Oh, for God's sake, Will.

WILL
Oh, come on! You're not pinnin' this one on me. He left, I wanted to talk to him for another twenty minutes. I was havin' fun.

LAMBEAU
I told you to cooperate with these people.

WILL
C'mon, that guy was a fuckin' piece of work.

Will gets up and adopts a hypnotic persona in front of Lambeau.

WILL
(spooky voice)
Look into my eyes. I don't need therapy.

LAMBEAU

Get out, Will.

WILL

Okay . . . Don't forget to get another therapist for next
week.

LAMBEAU

That's enough.

Will is out the door. Lambeau turns to Tom.

TOM

I called Mel Weintraub this morning, to check availabi-
lity.

LAMBEAU

What's the point?

TOM

What do you want to do?

LAMBEAU

There is somebody . . .

TOM

Who is he?

LAMBEAU

He was my roommate in college.

■ INT. BUNKER HILL CAMPUS—DAY

*This is SEAN MAGUIRE'S Dying and Bereavement class. Emblazoned on
the door is ROOM 101. While the lecture hall could hold sixty students, there
are less than fifteen here today.*

*Sean Maguire lectures to the class in a resigned tone. Tired of teaching, tired of
life, he finds himself resigned to the tedium of teaching core classes to an indifferent student body.*

SEAN

Establishing trust is the most important component in
making breakthroughs with a patient. Why?
(beat)

SEAN

Maureen?

MAUREEN'S only response is an empty stare.

SEAN

Keep up the good work, Maureen. Vinnie?

VINNIE looks up.

VINNIE

Because trust is an important thing.

SEAN

Don't bullshit me, Vinnie. Didn't your brother give
you the notes? Okay. If a patient doesn't trust you then
they won't feel safe enough to be honest with you—
then there's no point to them being in therapy. It's like
saying, "Fine, come here and don't tell me a thing, but
go home feeling like you're doing something about
your problems—and give me my fifty bucks before you
leave, will ya!"

He looks around the room for approval. No one is listening.

SEAN

If you don't help them trust you, then there's no way
you'll get them to sleep with you. And that should
be the goal of any good therapist. Insecure women, you
know . . . nail 'em when they're vulnerable—that's always been my motto.

The students look up, somewhat stunned.

SEAN

See? I got Vinnie's attention.

Laughter. Sean starts to resume his lecture, when he notices LAMBEAU standing in the back of the room. There is an awkward moment.

SEAN

Gerry.

LAMBEAU

Sean.

SEAN
(to class)

Well, it seems we're in the presence of greatness. Professor Gerald Lambeau is a Field's Medal–winner. Combinatorial mathematics. Nineteen eighty-six.

The students stare blankly.

LAMBEAU

Hello.

SEAN

The Field's Medal is the Nobel prize for math.
(beat)
But it's only given out every four years.

A beat.

SEAN

Okay, that's all for today. Try and get through Fernald by Monday.

The class starts to pack up and file out. Lambeau approaches Sean who steps down from the lectern.

LAMBEAU

Good to see you.

SEAN

Good to see you.

LAMBEAU
Is there someplace we can talk?

CUT TO:

■ EXT. HARVARD SQUARE—NIGHT

Will and Skylar on their first date. They watch a street MAGICIAN doing tricks with a rabbit. The guy's tricks are pretty good, but his onstage persona could use some work. He is incessantly repeating the phrase, "This is the rabbit, the rabbit really does the tricks." Will gives Skylar a look and they move on.

CUT TO:

■ INT. TOY STORE—LATER

Will and Skylar walk into the small shop.

SKYLAR
I don't know, it was just kind of the boring suburban thing. Private school, Harvard, and now med school.
(beat)
I actually figured out that at the end of it, my brain will be worth a quarter of a million dollars. I shouldn't have told you that. . . .

WILL
I bet your parents were happy to pay.

SKYLAR
I was happy to pay. I inherited money.

WILL
Is Harvard gettin' all that money?

SKYLAR
Stanford. I'm leaving in June after I graduate.

WILL
So you just want to use me and go?

                              SKYLAR
        Well, I'm gonna experiment on you for my anatomy
        class, then go.

                               WILL
        In that case, fine.
                              (beat)
        Want to see my magic trick?

                              SKYLAR
        Sure.

Will pulls out a heaping HANDFUL OF CARAMELS.

                               WILL
        Now, I'm gonna make all these caramels disappear.

                              SKYLAR
        Okay . . .

*Will goes into all manner of hocus-pocus theatrics, then shakes his hand wildly.
The trick doesn't pan out and the caramels go flying all over the store. Skylar
laughs.*

                               WILL
        It works better when I have my rabbit.

CUT TO:

■ INT. LOCKOBER RESTAURANT—NIGHT

*Lambeau and Sean share a table at this exclusive restaurant. Sean seems slightly
out of place in his wrinkled sport coat.*

                             LAMBEAU
        I didn't see you at the reunion.

                               SEAN
        I've been busy.

                    LAMBEAU
You were missed.
                    (beat)
How long has it been since we've seen each other?

                    SEAN
Since Nancy died.

                    LAMBEAU
I'm sorry, that damn conference—

                    SEAN
I got your card.

■ INT. HARVARD SQUARE DINER: THE TASTY—NIGHT

A FRY COOK hands Will and Skylar a pair of CHEESEBURGERS.

                    SKYLAR
Have you ever seen *Annie Hall?*

                    WILL
No.

                    SKYLAR
Well, there's this part of the movie that's about how
there's always this tension on a first date, where both
people are thinking about what's going to happen with
the whole "good-night kiss" thing.

Will smiles.

                    WILL
I really don't "date" that much.

                    SKYLAR
                    (laughs)
You know what I mean. I know you've at least
thought about it.

                    WILL
No I haven't. . . .

SKYLAR

Yes you have. You were thinking you were gonna get a good-night kiss.

WILL
(mock protest)

No I wasn't. . . .

SKYLAR

Yes you were.

WILL

I was kinda hopin' to get "good-night laid" but . . . I'll take a kiss.

She laughs.

SKYLAR

Oh, you will?

WILL

No . . . I was hoping to get a kiss.

SKYLAR

Then why don't we just get it out of the way.

He looks at her.

WILL

Now?

Both of them have cheeseburger in their mouths.

SKYLAR

Yeah.

They kiss, mouths full of burger. It's nice. A beat.

SKYLAR

That had to be the worst good-night kiss . . .

Will laughs.

WILL

Hey, look lady, I'm just here for the free food.

She smiles.

SKYLAR

Free?

WILL

Yeah, I spent all my money on those caramels.

She laughs.

CUT TO:

■ **INT. LOCKOBER RESTAURANT—SAME**

Lambeau and Sean, having finished their meal. Lambeau has been pitching Sean.

SEAN

I've been busy, Gerry. I got a full schedule.

LAMBEAU

This kid's special, Sean. I've never seen anything like him.

SEAN

Not much free time, Gerry.

LAMBEAU

Have you ever heard of a man named Ramanujan?

Sean nods his head.

SEAN

Yeah.

LAMBEAU

He was alive over a hundred years ago. He was Indian. Dots, not feathers. . . .

Sean finishes the joke. Lambeau chuckles.

LAMBEAU

So this Ramanujan lived in a tiny hut in India. No formal education, no access to other works. But he came
across an old math book and from this basic text he was
able to extrapolate theories that had baffled mathemati-
cians for years.

SEAN

And he mailed it to Hardy—

LAMBEAU

That's right, Sean. He mailed it to a professor at Cambridge who immediately recognized the brilliance in his
work and brought Ramanujan to England.

SEAN

Where he contracted pneumonia and died at a young
age—

LAMBEAU

They worked together for the remainder of their lives,
producing some of the most exciting math theory ever
done. Ramanujan's genius was unparalleled, Sean. This
boy is like that. But he's very defensive, and I need someone who can get through to him.

SEAN

Why me?

LAMBEAU

I need someone with your kind of background.

SEAN

My kind of background?

LAMBEAU

You're from the same neighborhood. South Boston.

SEAN

He's from Southie? How many people did you try before you came to me?

                                LAMBEAU
                          (looks squarely at Sean)
Five.

Sean gives a slight, knowing smile.

                                SEAN
              Who? Barry, Henry, Rick . . .

Lambeau nods.

                                SEAN
              Not Rick? You didn't send him to Rick?

                                LAMBEAU
              Just meet with the boy once a week.

                                SEAN
              Can we do it at my office?

                                LAMBEAU
              That would be fine.

The waiter comes with the CHECK. Each man reaches for it.

                                LAMBEAU
              Sean, please.

                                SEAN
              I got it.

                                LAMBEAU
              It's on the college.

Sean relents.

CUT TO:

■ EXT. BUNKER HILL CAMPUS—MORNING

*Establishing shot of the red brick campus. Planes land at nearby Logan airport.
Will walks up the steps.*

CUT TO:

■ INT. SEAN'S OFFICE—DAY

Sean's office is comfortable. Books are stacked against the wall. There is a PAINTING on the wall behind Sean. Sean is seated behind a desk. Lambeau sits in a chair in the back of the room, next to Tom. A long beat passes; they wait.

> LAMBEAU
>
> Any vulnerability he senses he'll exploit.

> SEAN
>
> I'll be okay.

> LAMBEAU
>
> It's a poker game with this young man. Don't let him see what you've got.

Sean nods. Will walks in. They stand to greet him.

> LAMBEAU
>
> Hello, Will. Any trouble finding this place?

> WILL
>
> No.

> LAMBEAU
>
> Will, this is Sean Maguire. Sean, Will Hunting.

Sean and Will nod. An awkward moment as the four men stand.

> LAMBEAU
>
> Well, let's get started.

> WILL
>
> Yeah, let's let the healing begin.

Lambeau is slightly embarrassed. Sean smiles at Will's joke.

> SEAN
>
> Would you excuse us?

Tom.

SEAN

You too, Gerry.

Lambeau looks at Sean, surprised. Sean's stare is unwavering. After an awkward moment, Lambeau and Tom go, leaving Sean and Will alone. Will doesn't look at Sean for more than a second. He seems more interested in the room. There is a long silence as Sean watches Will.

SEAN

Hello, Will. I'm Sean Maguire.

A smile crosses Will's face as he walks to his chair and sits. He lights a cigarette. Sean continues to watch him. Finally—

SEAN

Where are you from in Southie?

WILL

Did you buy all these books retail, or do you send away for like a "shrink kit" that comes with all these volumes included?

SEAN

Have you read all these books, Will?

WILL

Probably not.

SEAN
(indicating a shelf)
How 'bout the ones on that shelf?

Will's eyes flicker up to the shelf for an instant.

WILL

Yeah, I read those.

SEAN

What did you think?

WILL

I'm not here for a fuckin' book report. They're your
books, why don't you read 'em?

SEAN

I did.

WILL

That must have taken you a long time.

SEAN

Yeah, it did take me a long time.

*Sean says this with pride. His determined stare and confident manner catch Will
a bit off guard. Will rises from his chair and goes to the shelf.*

WILL
(looking at a book)
A History of the United States, Volume I. If you want to
read a real history book, read Howard Zinn's *A People's
History of the United States.* That book will knock you
on your ass. You people baffle me. You spend all this
money on beautiful, fancy books—and they're the
wrong fuckin' books.

SEAN

You think so?

WILL

Whatever blows your hair back.

Will returns to his chair. Pause.

SEAN
(indicating cigarette)
Guy your age shouldn't smoke so much. Stunt your
growth.

WILL

You're right. It really gets in the way of my jazzerciz-
ing.

*Sean does not seem at all affected by Will's attitude. He remains behind the big
desk with almost a half smile on his face. Will is aware of Sean's confidence.*

WILL

Do you lift?

SEAN

Yes, I do.

WILL

Nautilus?

SEAN

Free weights.

WILL

Oh yeah? Me, too. What do you bench?

SEAN

Two eighty-five.

WILL

Oh.

*Will gets up again and moves around his chair to Sean's painting. It is a picture
of an old sailboat in a tremendous storm—by no means a masterpiece. Will
studies it.*

WILL

You paint this?

SEAN

Yeah. Do you paint?

WILL

No.

SEAN

Crayons?

WILL

This is a real piece of shit.

SEAN

Tell me what you really think.

WILL

Poor color composition, lousy use of space. But that shit doesn't really concern me.

SEAN

What does?

WILL

The color here, see how dark it is? It's interesting.

SEAN

What is?

WILL

I think you're one step away from cutting your ear off. You ever hear the saying "Any port in a storm"?

SEAN

Sure, how 'bout "Still waters run deep"—

WILL

—Well, maybe that means you.

SEAN

Maybe what mea—

WILL

Maybe you were in the middle of a storm, a big fuckin' storm—the waves were crashing over the bow, the goddamned mast was about to snap and you were cryin' for the harbor. So you did what you had to, to get out. Maybe you became a psychologist.

                              SEAN
                Maybe you should be a patient and sit down.

                              WILL
                Maybe you married the wrong woman.

                              SEAN
                Watch your mouth.

                              WILL
                That's it, isn't it? You married the wrong woman. She
                leave you? Was she bangin' someone else?

Sean is walking slowly toward Will.

                              WILL
                How are the seas now, D—

In a flash, Sean has Will by the throat. Will is helpless.

                              SEAN
                If you ever disrespect my wife again . . . I will end you.

                            WILL
        Time's up.

CUT TO:

■ INT. HALLWAY—CONTINUOUS

Will walks out of Sean's office past Lambeau and Tom, who are sitting in the hallway.

                            WILL
        At ease, gentleman.

CUT TO:

■ INT. SEAN'S OFFICE—DAY

Sean stands behind the desk in his office, still very much on edge. Lambeau walks in.

                         LAMBEAU
        Five minutes, Sean. Are you okay?

A pause. Sean is staring at his painting.

                         LAMBEAU
        I'll understand if you don't want to meet with him
        again.

                          SEAN
        Thursday, four o'clock. Make sure the kid is here.

CUT TO:

■ EXT. WONDERLAND RACETRACK—DAY

Will and Skylar sit in the stands watching the dogs run. They ad lib teasing one another about England, Ireland and America.

                         SKYLAR
        So you grew up around here?

                    WILL
Not far from here, South Boston.

                    SKYLAR
How was that?

                    WILL
Pretty boring, I guess.

She smiles.

                    SKYLAR
I bet you have a great family.

                    WILL
You know, nothing special.

                    SKYLAR
You have a lot of brothers and sisters?

                    WILL
Do I have a lot of brothers and sisters?

                    SKYLAR
Yeah.

                    WILL
Well, Irish Catholic. What do you think?

                    SKYLAR
How many?

                    WILL
You wouldn't believe me if I told you.

                    SKYLAR
What, five?

Will shakes his head.

SKYLAR

Seven?

Will shakes his head. Smiles.

SKYLAR

Come on.

WILL

I have twelve big brothers.

SKYLAR

Not a chance.

WILL

Yup, you're lookin' at lucky thirteen.

SKYLAR

Bullshit.

WILL

I swear to God.

SKYLAR

Your house must have been a zoo.

WILL

It was great. There was always someone to play with, give you advice.

SKYLAR

Do you know all their names?

WILL

Course I do, they're my brothers.

SKYLAR

Well?

WILL

Marky, Ricky, Danny, Terry, Mikey, Davey, Timmy, Tommy, Joey, Robby, Johnny and Brian.

SKYLAR
(laughing)
Do you keep in touch with them?

WILL
All the time. We all live in Southie. I live with three of
'em now.

Skylar smiles.

SKYLAR
I want to meet them.

WILL
We'll do that.

CUT TO:

■ INT. SEAN'S APARTMENT—NIGHT

*As we pan across Sean's small apartment, we find it strewn with dirty clothes
and the sink full of dishes. If it weren't for all the clutter, the place would feel
pretty bare. A framed SPORTS ILLUSTRATED cover featuring a screaming
Larry Bird and titled "CELTIC PRIDE" hangs on the wall. Sean sits at the
table next to another nearly empty bottle of GENERIC'S IRISH WHISKY.
He is deep in thought.*

CUT TO:

■ INT. SEAN'S OFFICE—DAY

*Will strolls into the office. Sean is waiting there behind his desk. He seems dif-
ferent: more calm. Will and Sean stare at each other for a long moment.*

WILL
You again. How's the paintin' coming?

Sean stands up.

SEAN
Come with me.

CUT TO:

■ EXT. BOSTON COMMON—MINUTES LATER

Sean and Will sit in the bleachers in the mostly empty park. They look out over a small pond, on which a group of schoolchildren on a field trip ride the famous swan boats.

> WILL
> So what's with this place? You have a swan fetish? Is this something you'd like to talk about?

> SEAN
> I was thinking about what you said to me the other day, about my painting. I stayed up half the night thinking about it, and then something occurred to me and I fell into a deep, peaceful sleep and haven't thought about you since. You know what occurred to me?

> WILL
> No.

You're just a boy. You don't have the faintest idea
what you're talking about.

Why, thank you.

You've never been out of Boston.

No.

So if I asked you about art you could give me the
skinny on every art book ever written . . . Michelan-
gelo?

(beat)

You know a lot about him I bet. Life's work, criti-
cisms, political aspirations. But you couldn't tell me
what it smells like in the Sistine Chapel. You've never
stood there and looked up at that beautiful ceiling. And
if I asked you about women I'm sure you could give
me a syllabus of your personal favorites, and maybe
you've been laid a few times, too. But you couldn't tell
me how it feels to wake up next to a woman and be
truly happy. If I asked you about war you could refer
me to a bevy of fictional and nonfictional material, but
you've never been in one. You've never held your best
friend's head in your lap and watched him draw his last
breath, looking to you for help. And if I asked you
about love I'd get a sonnet, but you've never looked at
a woman and been truly vulnerable. Known that someone could kill you with a look. That someone could
rescue you from your grief. That God had put an angel
on earth just for you. And you wouldn't know how it
felt to be her angel. To have the love to be there for
her forever. Through anything, through cancer. You
wouldn't know about sleeping sitting up in a hospital
room for two months holding her hand and not leaving
because the doctors could see in your eyes that the term
visiting hours didn't apply to you. And you wouldn't
know about real loss, because that only occurs when

you lose something you love more than yourself, and you've never dared to love anything that much. I look at you and I don't see an intelligent, confident man; I don't see a peer, and I don't see my equal. I see a boy. Nobody could possibly understand you, right, Will? Yet you presume to know so much about me because of a painting you saw. You must know everything about me. You're an orphan, right?

Will nods quietly.

                         SEAN
Do you think I would presume to know the first thing about who you are because I read *Oliver Twist*? And I don't buy the argument that you don't want to be here, because I think you like all the attention you're getting. Personally, I don't care. There's nothing you can tell me that I can't read somewhere else. Unless we talk about your life. But you won't do that. Maybe you're afraid of what you might say.

Sean stands,

                         SEAN
    It's up to you.

and walks away.

CUT TO:

■ **INT. CONSTRUCTION SITE—DAY**

Will and Chuckie doing demo at the site. They throw cinder blocks out a window into a pile. They are filthy.

CUT TO:

■ **EXT. SOUTH BOSTON STREET—NIGHT**

Rain pounds South Boston. Chuckie sits with the Cadillac idling, humming to the radio. Morgan and Billy sit in the back, sharing a case of beer. Will is at a pay phone.

■ **INT. SKYLAR'S ROOM—NIGHT**

                         SKYLAR
Hello?

■ **EXT. SOUTH BOSTON STREET—NIGHT**

Will hangs up and runs back to the car, soaked.

                         CHUCKIE
Who'd you call?

                         WILL
No one. I didn't have the number.

                         MORGAN
What are you, retarded? You went all the way out
there in the rain and you didn't have the number?

                         WILL
No, it was your mother's nine hundred number. I just
ran out of quarters.

Laughter. Chuckie pulls away from the curb.

                         MORGAN
Why don't we get off mothers—I just got off yours.

*There is a long moment of silence in response to Morgan's attempt at levity.
Then laughter.*

                         BILLY
You're a pretty funny guy. Here, have a nickel.

*Billy WHIPS his EMPTY BEER CAN at Morgan and bounces it off his
head.*

                         MORGAN
Keep fuckin' with me. Watch what happens.

                         BILLY
All right, then.

                         MORGAN
Watch what happens.

CUT TO:

■ INT. SEAN'S OFFICE—DAY

Will sits across from Sean, completely silent, and takes out a pack of cigarettes.

> SEAN
>
> No smoking.

Will puts the cigarettes away. Sean stares at Will and occasionally at the clock. Sean continues to check the clock on the wall. It is the only clock in the room and it is BEHIND Will. Their hour is almost up.

■ CLOSE ON: WILL'S EYES INTERCUT WITH THE CLOCK

He is counting seconds. As the second hand crosses the twelve, Will stands up and walks out, leaving Sean alone.

■ INT. HALLWAY—LATER

Lambeau and Sean walk down the hallway after the session.

> LAMBEAU
>
> What do you mean, he didn't talk? You sat there for an hour?

> SEAN
>
> No, he just sat there and counted the seconds until the session was over. It was pretty impressive, actually.

> LAMBEAU
>
> Why would he do that?

> SEAN
>
> To show me he doesn't have to talk to me if he doesn't want to.

> LAMBEAU
>
> Oh, what is this? Some kind of staring contest between two kids from the "old neighborhood"?

> SEAN
>
> I won't talk first.

■ **EXT. WILL'S APARTMENT—EVENING**

Chuckie drops Will off at his apartment, watches him walk up the steps.

DISSOLVE TO:

■ **EXT. WILL'S APARTMENT—MORNING**

Chuckie pulls up to the curb and walks up the steps to Will's front door. After a beat, Will emerges. They get back in the car.

CUT TO:

■ **EXT. CONSTRUCTION SITE—DAY**

Will and Chuckie at work. Chuckie shows Will how to be a man.

■ **INT. L STREET BAR & GRILLE, SOUTH BOSTON—NIGHT**

The bar is a bit more crowded than usual. Will and Chuckie walk back to their table, carrying beers. They pass a table of GIRLS, local regulars getting just as bombed as the guys. These girls are a little overdone. Too much makeup, too much hairspray and too much body for such tight outfits. One of the girls, KRYSTYN, smiles at Will, who seems subdued.

KRYSTYN

Hi, Will.

WILL

How you doin', Krystyn?

They pass the table of girls. Chuckie looks at one, ruefully.

CHUCKIE

I didn't get on Cathy last night.

WILL

Why not?

CHUCKIE

I don't know.

Chuckie turns back to the table of girls, calling out:

> CHUCKIE
> Cathy! Why didn't you give me none of your twat last
> night?

A girl at the table, CATHY, holds up her PINKY FINGER and smiles, revealing a mouthful of MISSING TEETH.

> CATHY
> Fuck you and your Irish curse, Chuckie!

> CHUCKIE
> She's missin' teeth, Will.

Will nods, not really into it tonight.

> CHUCKIE
> Plus, it's like, five to two Morgan ends up marryin' her.
> There's only so many times you can bang your friend's
> future wife . . .

They get to the table. Will's heart just isn't in it.

> WILL
> I'm takin' off.

> ALL
> We're goin' late night.

> WILL
> I'm tired.

CUT TO:

■ INT. LAMBEAU'S OFFICE—DAY

Will and Lambeau work together at the board. They communicate nonverbally as they collaborate on a problem. After a particularly amusing series of numbers, they share a look and laugh.

CUT TO:

■ **INT. SEAN'S OFFICE—DAY**

Will and Sean sit in silence. A long moment passes. Sean casually reclines in his chair, disinterested. Will restlessly looks around the room and then back to Sean. An odd half smile crosses Sean's face. After a moment:

> **WILL**
>
> You know, I was on this plane once. And I'm sittin' there and the captain comes on and is like, "We'll be cruising at thirty-five thousand feet," and does his thing, then he puts the mike down but forgets to turn it off. Then he says, "Man, all I want right now is a blow job and a cup of coffee." So the stewardess goes runnin' up toward the cockpit to tell him the mike's still on, and this guy in the back of the plane goes, "Don't forget the coffee!"

> **SEAN**
> *(smiles)*
> You've never been on a plane.

> **WILL**
>
> I know, but the joke's better if I tell it in the first person.

A beat.

> **WILL**
>
> I have been laid, you know.

Sean smiles.

> **SEAN**
>
> Yeah? You got a lady now?

> **WILL**
>
> Yeah, I went on a date last week.

> **SEAN**
>
> How'd it go?

                    WILL
Fine.

                    SEAN
Well, are you going out again?

                    WILL
I don't know.

                    SEAN
Why not?

                    WILL
Haven't called her.

                    SEAN
Jesus Christ, you are an amateur.

                    WILL
I know what I'm doing. She's different from the other
girls I met. We have a really good time. She's smart,
beautiful, fun . . .

SEAN

So Christ, call her up.

WILL

Why? So I can realize she's not so smart? That she's boring? You don't get it. Right now she's perfect. I don't want to ruin that.

SEAN

And right now you're perfect, too. Maybe you don't want to ruin that.

Will says nothing.

SEAN

Well, I think that's a great philosophy, Will. That way you can go through your entire life without ever having to really know anybody.

Sean looks directly at Will, who looks away. A beat.

SEAN

My wife used to turn the alarm clock off in her sleep. I was late for work all the time because in the middle of the night she'd roll over and turn the damn thing off. Eventually I got a second clock and put it under my side of the bed, but it got to where she was gettin' to that one, too. She was afraid of the dark, so the closet light was on all night. Thing kept me up half the night. Eventually I'd fall asleep out of sheer exhaustion, and not wake up when I was supposed to 'cause she'd have already gotten to my alarms.

Will smiles, Sean takes a beat.

SEAN

My wife's been dead two years, Will. And when I think about her, those are the things I think about most. Little idiosyncrasies that only I knew about. Those made her my wife. And she had the goods on me, too. Little things I do out of habit. People call these things imperfections, Will. It's just who we are. And we get to choose who we're going to let into our own weird little worlds. You're not perfect. And let me save you the suspense—this girl you met isn't, either. The question is whether or not you're perfect for each other. You can know everything in the world, but the only way you're findin' that one out is by giving it a shot. You sure won't get the answer from an old fucker like me. And even if I did know, I wouldn't tell you.

Will smiles. A beat.

                    WILL
Why not? You told me every other fuckin' thing. You talk more than any shrink I ever met.

Sean laughs.

                    SEAN
I teach this shit, I didn't say I knew how to do it.

                    WILL
You ever think about gettin' remarried?

                    SEAN
My wife's dead.

                    WILL
Hence, the word remarried.

                    SEAN
My wife's dead.

                    WILL
Well I think that's a wonderful philosophy, Sean. That way you can go through the rest of your life without having to really know anyone.

A beat. Sean smiles.

                    SEAN
    Time's up.

CUT TO:

■ **EXT. SKYLAR'S DORM—AFTERNOON**

Will is waiting outside the door for someone to come out so he can go in.

CUT TO:

■ **INT. SKYLAR'S DORM—AFTERNOON**

The door to Skylar's dorm is partially open. Will stands outside while Skylar remains on the threshold.

> SKYLAR
> Where have you been?

> WILL
> I'm sorry, I been real busy.

> SKYLAR
> You were busy? You know, I really was waiting for you to call me.

> WILL
> Sorry. I'm sorry. Give me another crack at it. Let me take you out.

> SKYLAR
> You should have called. I have an O-Chem lab due to-morrow and it's impossible.
> *(beat)*
> It's not an excuse, dummy. I want to go out with you. But look:

She holds up her lab. Will glances at it.

> SKYLAR
> Tomorrow?

> WILL
> Promise?

SKYLAR
If you bring the caramels.

Will smiles.

CUT TO:

■ **EXT. HARVARD SQUARE—LATER**

Will sits in an outdoor café, thinking. After a beat, he leans over to two students working at a nearby table, borrows a pen and paper and starts writing.

CUT TO:

■ **EXT. SKYLAR'S DORM—DAY**

Will is a solitary figure strolling across the lawn. He stops at Skylar's dorm and knocks on the door.

CUT TO:

■ **INT. SKYLAR'S DORM—DAY**

She emerges. He hands her the paper he was working on. It is her O-Chem lab.

WILL
I couldn't wait till tomorrow.

SKYLAR
How the hell did you do that?

WILL
Didn't your mother ever tell you not to look a gift
horse in the mouth?

SKYLAR
I'm supposed to understand this.

WILL
You're not going into surgery tomorrow, are you?

SKYLAR
No.

                    WILL
Then let's go have some fun.

With a smile, she relents.

■ **INT. SEAN'S OFFICE—DAY**

Sean and Will in session.

                    SEAN
Really? How'd the date go?

                    WILL
Do you still counsel veterans?
                    (beat)
I read your book last night.

                    SEAN
No, I don't.

                    WILL
Why not?

                    SEAN
I gave that up when my wife got sick.

                    WILL
Is that why you didn't write anything else?

                    SEAN
                    (smiles)
I didn't write anything else 'cause nobody, including
most of my colleagues, bothered to read the first one.

                    WILL
Well, I've read your colleagues. Your book was good,
Sean.
                    (beat)
All those guys were in your platoon?

                    SEAN
Yeah.

WILL

What happened to that guy from Kentucky?

SEAN

Lon? He got married. He has a kid. I kind of lost touch
with him after Nancy got sick.

WILL

Do you ever wonder what your life would be like if
you never met your wife?

SEAN

What? Do I wonder if I'd be better off if I never met
my wife?

Will starts to clarify his question.

SEAN

No, that's okay. It's an important question. 'Cause
you'll have your bad times, which wake you up to the
good stuff you weren't paying attention to. And you
can fail, as long as you're trying hard. But there's nothing worse than regret.

WILL

You don't regret meetin' your wife?

SEAN

Why? Because of the pain I feel now? I have regrets,
Will, but I don't regret a single day I spent with her.

WILL

When did you know she was the one?

SEAN

October twenty-first, nineteen seventy-five. Game six
of the World Series. Biggest game in Red Sox history.
Me and my friends slept out on the sidewalk all night
to get tickets. We were sitting in a bar waiting for the
game to start, and in walks this girl. What a game that
was. Tie game in the bottom of the twelfth inning, in
steps Carlton Fisk, hits a long fly ball down the left field
line. Thirty-five thousand fans on their feet, screamin'
at the ball to stay fair.

Fisk is runnin' up the baseline, wavin' at the ball like a madman. It hits the foul pole, home run. Thirty-five thousand people went crazy. And I wasn't one of them.

                    WILL

Where were you?

                    SEAN

I was havin' a drink with my future wife.

                    WILL

You missed Pudge Fisk's home run to have a drink with a woman you had never met?

                    SEAN

That's right.

                    WILL

So wait a minute. The Red Sox haven't won a World Series since nineteen eighteen, you slept out for tickets, game's gonna start in twenty minutes, in walks a girl you never seen before and you give your ticket away?

                    SEAN

You should have seen this girl. She lit up the room.

                    WILL

I don't care if Helen of Troy walked into that bar! That's game six of the World Series!

Sean smiles.

                    WILL

And what kind of friends are these? They let you get away with that?

                    SEAN

I just slid my ticket across the table and said, "Sorry fellas, I gotta go see about a girl."

                    WILL

"I gotta go see about a girl"? What did they say?

SEAN

They could see that I meant it.

WILL

You're kiddin' me.

SEAN

No, Will, I'm not kiddin' you. If I had gone to see that game I'd be in here talkin' about a girl I saw at a bar twenty years ago. And how I always regretted not goin' over there and talkin' to her. I don't regret the eighteen years we were married. I don't regret givin' up counseling for six years when she got sick. I don't regret being by her side for the last two years when things got real bad. And I sure as hell don't regret missing that damn game.

A beat. Will is impressed.

WILL

Would have been nice to catch that game, though.

SEAN
(breaking)
Well hell, I didn't know Pudge was gonna hit the home run.

They laugh.

TIME DISSOLVE TO:

■ INT. LAMBEAU'S OFFICE—DAY

The office is more crowded than usual. TOM and THREE of LAMBEAU'S COLLEAGUES including the esteemed ALEXANDER PEKEC are in the room. Will sits at a workstation, which projects a proof of his onto the chalkboard. Lambeau stands beside the projected image at the board, arguing with Pekec, a foreign mathematician. The image is of a Ramses graph binary tree.

LAMBEAU
The boy has found a simple geometric picture.

PEKEC
A tree structure won't work!

LAMBEAU
Look, he's joining the two vertices.

Pekec starts writing lines beside Will's proof on the board.

PEKEC
But I can do the sum.

LAMBEAU
No, there's a limit.

PEKEC
The limit doesn't agree!

WILL
I can cut it into two irreducible parts.

PEKEC
There is no proof—

Lambeau can no longer contain himself.

LAMBEAU
—It's how you group the terms.

PEKEC
—But—

WILL
Look, I wrote it down.

They turn to Will, who places his proof on the projector. The image is cast over their faces.

As Pekec reads and the realization dawns on him:

WILL
It's just simpler this way.

Lambeau turns with satisfaction to an understanding Pekec.

LAMBEAU

Alexander, your theory has been superseded.

CUT TO:

■ INT. SKYLAR'S ROOM—NIGHT

Will and Skylar in her room, postcoital. They are wrapped in a sheet. Will is absentmindedly playing the memory game SIMON. The pattern grows increasingly complex. After a beat:

SKYLAR

Why do we always stay here?

WILL

'Cause it's nicer than my place.

SKYLAR

I've never seen your place.

WILL

Exactly.

SKYLAR

What about your friends? Or your brothers? When do I
get to meet them?

WILL

They don't come over here that much.

SKYLAR

I think I can make it to South Boston.

WILL

Aah, it's kind of a hike.

SKYLAR

Is it me you're hiding from them or the other way
around?

WILL

All right, all right. We'll go.

SKYLAR

When?

WILL

Sometime. I don't know. Next week.

SKYLAR

What if I said I wouldn't sleep with you again until you
let me meet your friends?

WILL

I'd say . . .
                    (reaches for phone)
It's only four in the mornin', they're prob'ly up.

She laughs. Stops him.

SKYLAR

You men are shameful. If you're not thinking with
your weiner then you're acting on its behalf.

WILL
Then on behalf of my weiner, I'd like to ask for an advance.

CUT TO:

■ INT. L STREET BAR & GRILLE—LATER

Skylar and Will sit together, along with Will's gang. The boys are considerably drunk, but it makes for good entertainment. Everyone here is having fun, including Skylar.

MORGAN
Will, I can't believe you brought Skylar here when we're all wrecked. What's she gonna think about us?

WILL
Yeah, Morgan. It's a real rarity that we'd be out drinkin'.

BILLY
I've been shit-faced for like two weeks.

MORGAN
Oh great, tell her that! Now she really thinks we're problem drinkers!

CHUCKIE
Two weeks? That's nothin'. My Uncle Marty? Will knows him. That guy fuckin' drinks like you've never seen!

CHUCKIE
One night he was drivin' back to his house on I Ninety-three, statie pulls him over.

ALL
Oh, shit.

CHUCKIE
Guy's tryin' to walk the line—but he can't even fuckin' stand up, and so my uncle's gonna spend a night in jail.

Just then there's this fuckin' *BOOM*, like fifty yards down the road. Some guy's car hit a tree.

                    MORGAN
Some other guy?

                    CHUCKIE
Yeah, he was probably drunker than my uncle, who fuckin' knows? So the cop goes, "Stay here," and he goes runnin' down the highway to deal with the other crash. So, my Uncle Marty's standin' on the side of the road for a little while, and he's so fuckin' lit that he forgets what he's waitin' for. So he goes, "Fuck it." He gets in his car and drives home.

                    MORGAN
Holy shit.

                    CHUCKIE
So in the morning there's a knock on the door. It's the statie. So my uncle's like, "Is there a problem?" And statie's like, "I pulled you over and you took off." And my uncle's like, "I never seen you before in my life. I been home all night with my kids." And statie's like, "Let me get in your garage!" So he's like, "All right, fine." He takes him around the garage and opens the door—and the statie's cruiser is in my uncle's garage.

                    ALL
No way! You're kiddin'!

                    CHUCKIE
No, he was so hammered that he drove the police cruiser home. Fuckin' lights and everything!

                    MORGAN
Did your uncle get arrested?

CHUCKIE

The fuckin' trooper was so embarrassed he didn't do anything. The fuckin' guy had been drivin' around in my
uncle's car all night, lookin' for the house!

Everyone is laughing. Skylar speaks above the din.

SKYLAR

There was this Irish guy, walking down the beach one
day.

She has everyone's attention. Will is nervous.

SKYLAR

And he came across a bottle, and this genie pops out.
The genie turned to the Irishman and says, "You've re-
leased me from my prison, so I'll grant you three
wishes." The Irish guy thinks for a minute and says,
"What I really want is a pint of Guiness that never
empties." And—*POOF!* A bottle appears. He slams it
down, and—lo and behold—it fills back up again.

C/U of Will. Hoping the joke pans out.

SKYLAR

Well, the Irish guy can't believe it. He drinks it again,
and again—*BOOM!* It fills back up. So, while the Irish
guy is marveling at his good fortune, The genie is getting impatient, because it's hot and he wants to get on
with his freedom. He says, "Let's go. You have two
more wishes." The Irish guy slams his drink again, it
fills back up, he's still amazed. The genie can't take it
anymore. He says, "Buddy, I'm boiling out here. What
are your other two wishes?"
> (beat)

The Irish guy looks at his drink, looks at the genie and
says . . . "I guess I'll have two more of these."

The gang erupts with laughter.

CHUCKIE

It's a good thing no one's Irish here.

MORGAN

I'm Irish.

Chuckie, Will look at Morgan, baffled.

■ **EXT. L STREET BAR & GRILLE—LATER**

*Everyone is walking out, saying good-bye. Chuckie goes over to Will and Sky-
lar.*

CHUCKIE

I'm glad you came by; changed my opinion of Harvard
people.

SKYLAR

See ya, Chuckie. I had fun.

Chuckie heads toward Will to say good night.

WILL

I don't know what the fuck you're doin'. You're givin'
us a ride.

CHUCKIE

What do I look like, Al Cowling?
(*seriously*)
You want to take my car, drop her off?

WILL

I was countin' on it.

MORGAN

Chuck, let's go.

CHUCKIE

You're walkin', bitch, Will's takin' the car.

*Morgan mumbles something and staggers off. Billy follows with an indifferent
shrug.*

WILL

Thanks, Chuck.

CHUCKIE

Don't get too happy. You're takin' me home first.

WILL

I don't know, Chuck. It's kinda outta the way.

CHUCKIE

Just 'cause you don't have to sleep in the one-room
palace, don't start thinkin' you're bad.

SKYLAR
(to Will)

I thought you said you'd show me your place.

WILL

Not tonight.

CHUCKIE

Yeah, not tonight. Not any other night. He knows,
once you see that shit-hole he's gettin' dropped like a
bad habit.

SKYLAR

I wanted to meet your brothers. . . .

Chuckie gives Will a curious look.

WILL

They're all sleepin' now.
(a beat, to Chuckie)
Let me get those keys.

CUT TO:

■ **INT. FACULTY CLUB—NIGHT** ·

*A cocktail party is underway. Professors mingle with representatives from
high-tech companies. Lambeau stands, holding a drink and surrounded by several
RECRUITERS. Apparently he's the star of the show.*

RECRUITER #1

What I want to know, Gerry, is when we get to meet
this wonder boy.

LAMBEAU

We're still working together, the boy's a little rough.

RECRUITER #2

We've got our share of eccentric geniuses at McNeil.
We know how to deal with that.

RECRUITER #3

I think we all do.

Laughter.

RECRUITER #1

If you're not exaggerating, Gerry—

LAMBEAU

Was I exaggerating in nineteen eighty-four when I told
you I'd win the Field's Medal within two years?

More laughter.

RECRUITER #1

In that case, the boy could run shipping for us, routing—

RECRUITER #2

You say he doesn't have a diploma, but we'll—

RECRUITER #1

I don't need to see a driver's license. I can think of
three departments right now that he could head up for
us.

LAMBEAU

At ease, gentlemen. We're looking carefully at all our
options.

RECRUITER #3

All right, Gerry. Close to the vest.
                (gives him his card)
Good luck with these vultures.

He walks off.

CUT TO:

■ INT. TIMMY'S TAP—DAY

Timmy's Tap is a local watering hole, not unlike the L Street. Sean is at the bar, telling a joke to TIMMY, forty-five, the owner of the place, and several other REGULARS.

> SEAN
>
> So she goes runnin' up the aisle and I figure, fuck it, and I yell out, "Don't forget the coffee!"

The men erupt in laughter. MARTY, one of the regulars, pipes up.

> MARTY
>
> Bullshit! You didn't say that!

Timmy and Sean exchange a look.

> TIMMY
>
> Jesus Christ, Marty. It's a joke.

Lambeau enters, a bit overdressed in his sport coat and tie.

> SEAN
>
> Gerry! Any trouble finding the place?

> LAMBEAU
>
> Not at all.

> SEAN
>
> Timmy, this is Gerry, an old friend of mine. We went to college together.

> TIMMY
>
> Good to meet you.

> LAMBEAU
>
> Pleasure to meet you.

> SEAN
>
> Could we get a couple of sandwiches?
> *(beat, smiles)*

Put it on my tab.

Sean heads toward a table.

TIMMY
You ever plan on payin' your tab?

SEAN
(pulls out lottery ticket)
I got the winning number right here.

TIMMY
What's the jackpot?

SEAN
Twelve million.

TIMMY
I don't think that'll cover it.

Lambeau follows. They sit.

LAMBEAU
You're here quite a bit, then.

SEAN
I live right around the corner.

LAMBEAU
You moved?

SEAN
I been here a couple years.

There is an awkward moment.

SEAN
You wanted to talk about Will?

LAMBEAU
Seems like it's going well.

                          SEAN
I think so.

                        LAMBEAU
Well, have you talked to him at all about his future?

                          SEAN
We haven't really gotten into it.

                        LAMBEAU
Maybe you should. My phone's been ringing off the
hook with job offers.

                          SEAN
Jobs doing what?

                        LAMBEAU
Cutting edge mathematics.
                          (beat)
Think tanks. The kind of place where a mind like
Will's is given free rein.

                          SEAN
That's great, Gerry, that there's interest . . . But I'm not
sure he's ready for that.

                        LAMBEAU
Sean, I really don't think you understand—

                          SEAN
What don't I understand?

Timmy comes over with the sandwiches.

                          SEAN
Thanks, Timmy.

                        LAMBEAU
Excuse me, Timmy. Could you help us? We're trying
to settle a bet.

                          TIMMY
Uh-oh.

LAMBEAU

Have you ever heard of Jonas Salk?

TIMMY

Yeah, cured polio.

LAMBEAU

You've heard of Albert Einstein?

Timmy smiles. Gives him a look.

LAMBEAU

How about Gerald Lambeau? Ever heard of him?

TIMMY

No.

LAMBEAU

Okay. Thank you, Timmy.

TIMMY

So who won the bet?

LAMBEAU

I did.

A beat. Timmy leaves.

LAMBEAU

This isn't about me. I'm nothing compared to this
young man.
                            (beat)
Sean, in nineteen-oh-five there were hundreds of professors who were renowned for their study of the uni-
verse. But it was a twenty-six-year-old Swiss patent
clerk, doing physics in his spare time, who changed the
world, Sean. Can you imagine if Einstein had given
that up? Or gotten drunk with his buddies in Vienna
every night? All of us would have lost something. And
I'm quite sure Timmy never would have heard of him.

SEAN

Isn't that a little dramatic, Gerry?

LAMBEAU

No, Sean. This boy has that gift. He just hasn't got the direction. We can give that to him.

A beat.

SEAN

He married his cousin.

LAMBEAU

Who?

SEAN

Einstein. Had two marriages, both train wrecks. The guy never saw his kids, one of whom, I think, ended up in an asylum—

LAMBEAU

You see, Sean? That's exactly not the point. No one remembers that. They—

SEAN

I do.

LAMBEAU

Well, you're the only one.
(beat)
This boy can make contributions to the world. We can help him do that.

SEAN

Just . . . take it easy, Gerry.

LAMBEAU

Look, I don't know what else I can say. I'm not sitting at home every night, twisting my mustache and hatching a plan to ruin the boy's life. But it's important to start early. I was doing advanced mathematics at eighteen and it still took me twenty-three years to do something worthy of a Field's Medal.

                    SEAN
Maybe he doesn't care about that.

A beat.

                    LAMBEAU
Sean, this is important. And it's above personal rivalry—

                    SEAN
Now wait a minute, Gerry—

                    LAMBEAU
No, no, you hear me out, Sean. This young man is a
true prodigy—

                    SEAN
—Personal rivalry? I'm not gettin' back at you

                    LAMBEAU
Look, you took one road and I took another. That's
fine.

                    SEAN
Is it, Gerry? 'Cause I don't think it's fine with you.
Give him time to figure out what he wants.

                    LAMBEAU
That's a wonderful theory, Sean. It worked wonders for
you.

A beat. Lambeau gets up.

                    LAMBEAU
Sean, I came here today out of courtesy. I wanted to
keep you in the loop. As we speak, the boy is in a
meeting I set up for him over at McNeil.

CUT TO:

■ INT. MCNEIL LABORATORIES, OFFICE—SAME

Three well-dressed McNeil EXECUTIVES sit around a conference table, which is littered with promotional brochures. The executives exchange a confused look. One of them speaks.

EXECUTIVE #1
(tentative)

Well, Will, I'm not exactly sure what you mean. We've already offered you a position . . .

Cut to reveal: Chuckie sitting across from the executives, hair combed down, wearing his Sunday best.

CHUCKIE

Since this is obviously not my first time in such altercations, let me say this:

Chuckie rubs the tips of his fingers together, indicating "cash." The executives are baffled.

CHUCKIE

Look, we can do this the easy way or the hard way.

The executives are completely blank.

CHUCKIE

At the current time I am looking at a number of different fields from which to disseminate which offer is most pursuant aid to my benefit.
(beat)
What do you want? What do I want? What does anybody want? Leniency.

EXECUTIVE #2

I'm not sure—

102

CHUCKIE

—These circumstances are mitigated. Right now. They're mitigated.

Chuckie puts his hands up, as if getting a vibe from the room.

EXECUTIVE #1

Okay . . .

Chuckie points to the third executive.

CHUCKIE

He knows what I'm talkin' about.

The third executive is baffled.

CHUCKIE

A retainer. Nobody in this town works without a retainer. You think you can find someone who does, you have my blessin'. But I think we all know that person isn't goin' to represent you as well as I can.

EXECUTIVE #2

Will, our offer starts you at eighty-four thousand a year, plus benefits.

CHUCKIE

Retainer . . .

EXECUTIVE #2

You want us to give you cash right now?

CHUCKIE

Allegedly, what I am saying is your situation will be concurrently improved if I had two hundred sheets in my pocket right now.

The executives exchange looks and go for their wallets.

EXECUTIVE #1

I don't think I . . . Larry?

EXECUTIVE #2

I have about seventy-three . . .

EXECUTIVE #1

Will you take a check?

CHUCKIE

Come now . . . What do you think I am, a juvenile?
You don't got any money on you right now. You
think I'm gonna take a check?

EXECUTIVE #3

It's fine, John, I can cover the rest.

CHUCKIE

That's right, you know.
(turns to #1)
He knows.

Chuckie stands up and takes the money.

CHUCKIE
(to #1)
You're suspect.
(beat)
I don't know what your reputation is, but after the shit
you tried to pull today, you can bet I'll be looking into
it. Any conversations you want to have with me
heretofore, you can have with my aforementioned at-
torney. Gentlemen, keep your ears to the grindstone.

CUT TO:

■ **EXT. AU BON PAIN COURTYARD, HARVARD SQUARE—DAY**

*Will and Skylar sit in the open courtyard of this Harvard Square eatery. Skylar
is working on another O-Chem lab. Will sits across from her, slightly bored,
watching her work.*

WILL

How's it goin'?

SKYLAR

Fine.

WILL

Want me to take a look?

SKYLAR

No.

WILL

C'mon, give me a peek and we'll go to the battin'
cages.

SKYLAR

It's important that I learn this.

WILL

Why is that important to you? If I inherited all that
money, the only thing important to me would be workin' on my swing.

SKYLAR

Clearly.

WILL

You're rich. What do you have to worry about?

SKYLAR

Rich? I have an inheritance. It's two hundred and fifty
thousand dollars. That's exactly what it'll cost me, mi-
nus about five hundred bucks, to go all the way
through med school. This is what I'm doing with that
money. I could have done anything I wanted. I could
have expanded my wardrobe, substantially.

WILL

Instead you're gonna bust your ass for five years so you
can be broke?

SKYLAR

No, so I can be a doctor.

A beat. Will nods. She looks down, then up.

SKYLAR

All right, Mr. Nosey Parker. Let me ask you a question? Do you have a photographic memory?

WILL

I guess. I don't know. How do you remember your phone number?

SKYLAR

Have you ever studied organic chemistry?

WILL

Some, a little.

SKYLAR

Just for fun?

WILL

I guess so.

SKYLAR

Nobody does organic chemistry for fun. It's necessary. Especially someone like you.

WILL

Like me?

SKYLAR

Yeah. Someone like you, who divides his time, fairly evenly, between the batting cages and bars.

Will laughs.

SKYLAR

How did you do that? I can't . . . I mean even the smartest people I know, and we do have a few at Harvard, have to study. A lot. It's hard.
                    (beat)
Listen, Will, if you don't want to tell me—

WILL

Do you play the piano?

SKYLAR

Come on, Will. I just want to know.

WILL

I'm tryin' to explain it to you. So you play the piano.
When you look at the keys, you see music, you see
Mozart.

SKYLAR

I see "Hot Cross Buns," but okay.

WILL

Well, all right: Beethoven. He looked at a piano and
saw music. The fuckin' guy was deaf when he com-
posed the *Ode to Joy*. They had to turn him around to
take a bow 'cause he didn't hear the crowd goin' crazy
behind him. Stone deaf. He saw all of that music in his
head.

SKYLAR

So, do you play piano?

WILL

Not a lick. I look at a piano and I see black and white
keys, three pedals and a box of wood. Beethoven, Mozart, they looked at it and it just made sense to them.
They saw a piano and they could play. I couldn't paint
you a picture, I probably can't hit the ball out of Fen-
way Park and I can't play the piano—

SKYLAR

But you can do my O-Chem lab in under an hour, you
can—

WILL

When it came to stuff like that I could always just play.

They kiss.

SKYLAR

I can't believe it's taken me four years to meet you and
I'm going to California in two months, Will.
(beat)
Have you ever been to California? I bet you'd like it.

Will freezes. A beat.

SKYLAR

Maybe not.

CUT TO:

■ **INT. CHUCKIE'S APARTMENT—DAY**

*Chuckie sits on his couch, watching cartoons in his boxers and a T-shirt, eating
cereal. The doorbell rings. He sits.*

CHUCKIE

Get it, Ma!

She doesn't. He gets up. Opens door. It's Skylar.

                              CHUCKIE
                             (surprised)
Hey.

                              SKYLAR
Hi.

                              CHUCKIE
How you doin'?

                              SKYLAR
Good.

An awkward beat.

                              CHUCKIE
How'd you know where to find me?

                              SKYLAR
                             (smiles)
You were the only Sullivan in the phone book.

Chuckie smiles.

                              SKYLAR
Will and I dropped you off here, remember?

                              CHUCKIE
Oh, right.

                              SKYLAR
This is your house, right?

*Chuckie nods and is about to respond when he is interrupted by a nagging shriek
from his mom.*

                           CHUCKIE'S MOM
Get in here, Chuckie!

                              CHUCKIE
                            (calling back)
Pipe down, Ma!

SKYLAR

I guess so.

CHUCKIE

What? No. This is my mother's house. I don't live with
my mother. I just stop by, help out. I'm good like that.

SKYLAR

Is this a bad time?

CHUCKIE

She'll live.
(beat)
If she starts yellin' again I might have to run in real
quick and beat her with the stick again but . . .

SKYLAR

Okay.

CHUCKIE

Let's take a walk.

■ EXT. CHUCKIE'S STREET—DAY

Chuckie, still in his boxers, walks with Skylar, who is talking.

SKYLAR

See, now this doesn't feel right.
(beat)
When I made the decision to come over here it felt
right. I had all these rationalizations. . . . I just don't understand why Will never tells me anything, he won't let
me get close to him, he tells me these weird lies—

CHUCKIE

You caught that, huh?

SKYLAR

I just wanted to find out what was going on. . . . But
now that I'm here it seems strange, doesn't it?

CHUCKIE
Well, I don't have no trousers on. . . .

She laughs. A beat.

CHUCKIE
I know why you're here. Will don't talk much.

SKYLAR
I don't care what his family's like or if he doesn't have
any brothers, but he doesn't have to lie to me.

CHUCKIE
I really don't know what to say. Look, I lie to women
all the time. That's just my way.
                    (beat)
Last week Morgan brought these girls down from Ros-
lindale. I told them I was a cosmonaut. They believed
me. But Will's not usually like that—

MAN ON PORCH
Put some clothes on, Sullivan!

CHUCKIE
Take it easy, Father!

She laughs.

CHUCKIE
All I can say is, I known Will a long time. And I seen
him with every girl he's ever been with. But I've never
seen him like this before, ever with anyone, like how
he is with you.

SKYLAR
Is that true?

CHUCKIE
Yeah. It is.

111

CUT TO:

■ INT. LAMBEAU'S OFFICE—DAY

Tom and Will are sitting waiting for Lambeau. There is a quiet moment as the two wait. Tom gives Will several looks, then speaks.

> **TOM**
> You know, Professor Lambeau is really quite a great man. A great man.

> **WILL**
> Okay, Tom.

> **TOM**
> I hope you appreciate what Professor Lambeau's been trying to do for you. Because I've been here through this whole process. I've been sitting here and I know how much he enjoys working with you, not against you.

Lambeau enters, going over a thick proof Will has completed.

> **LAMBEAU**
> This is correct. I see you used McClaren here—

> **WILL**
> I don't know what it's called.

> **LAMBEAU**
> —This can't be right.
> *(examining proof)*
> This is going to be very embarrassing. Have you ever considered—

> **WILL**
> I'm pretty sure it's right.

Will gets up to leave.

WILL
(turning back)
Can I ask you a favor—can we do this at Sean's from
now on? 'Cause I leave work to come here, and the
fuckin' commute is killin' me—

LAMBEAU
That's fine, but did you ever think—

WILL
It's right.
(beat, heading out)
Take it home with you.

LAMBEAU
Will, what happened at the McNeil meeting?

WILL
I couldn't go 'cause I had a date. So I sent my chief
negotiator.

LAMBEAU
Will, on your own time, you can do what you like.
When I set up a meeting with my associates and you
don't show up, it reflects poorly on me.

WILL
Then don't set up any more meetings.

LAMBEAU
I'll cancel every meeting right now. I'll give you a job
myself. I just wanted you to see what was out there.

WILL
—Maybe I don't want to spend my life sittin' around
and explaining shit to people.

LAMBEAU
The least you can do is show me a little appreciation.

WILL
(indicates proof)
—You know how fuckin' easy this is to me? This is a
joke!
(crumples proof)
And I'm sorry you can't do this. I really am. 'Cause if
you could I wouldn't be forced to watch you fumble
around and fuck it up.

LAMBEAU
Sure, then you'd have more time to sit around and get
drunk. Think of how many fights you could have been
in by now.

*Will turns around, revealing that he's lit the PROOF ON FIRE. Will drops
it on the floor. Lambeau drops to his knees and puts it out. He looks up at
Will.*

LAMBEAU
You're right, Will. I can't do that proof and you can.
And when it comes to this there are only twenty people in the world that can tell the difference between
you and me. But I'm one of them.

WILL
Well, I'm sorry.

LAMBEAU
So am I.
(beat)
Yes. That's right, Will. Most days I wish I never met
you. Because then I could sleep at night. I wouldn't
have to walk around with the knowledge that someone
like you was out there. And I wouldn't have to watch
you throw it all away.

*Lambeau gathers his composure and picks up the wrinkled proof. He stands up,
smooths it out.*

CUT TO:

■ INT. SKYLAR'S ROOM—NIGHT

Will and Skylar lie in bed. Skylar watches Will sleep. She gets up and goes to the fridge. Returning to the bed:

SKYLAR

Will? Are you awake?

WILL

No.

SKYLAR

Come with me to California.

WILL

What?

SKYLAR

I want you to come with me.

WILL

How do you know that?

SKYLAR

I know. I just do.

WILL

Yeah, but how do you know?

SKYLAR

I don't know. I just feel it.

WILL

And you're sure about that?

SKYLAR

Yeah. I'm sure.

WILL

'Cause that's a serious thing you're sayin'. I mean, we might be in California next week and you could find out somethin' about me that you don't like. And you might feel like, "Hey, this is a big mistake."
(getting upset)
But you can't take it back, 'cause you know it's real serious and you can't take somethin' like that back. Now I'm in California, 'cause you asked me to come. But you don't really want me there. And I'm stuck in California with someone who doesn't really want me there and just wishes they had a take-back.

SKYLAR

"Take-back?" What is that? I don't want a take-back. I want you to come to California with me.

WILL

I can't go out to California.

                    SKYLAR
Why not?

                    WILL
One, because I have a job here and two, because I live
here—

                    SKYLAR
                    (beat)
Look, Will, if you're not in love with me, you can say
that.

                    WILL
I'm not sayin' I'm not in love with you.

                    SKYLAR
Then what are you afraid of?

                    WILL
What do you mean, what am I afraid of?

                    SKYLAR
Why won't you come with me? What are you so
scared of?

                    WILL
What am I so scared of?

                    SKYLAR
Well, what aren't you scared of? You live in your safe
little world where nobody challenges you and you're
scared shitless to do anything else—

                    WILL
Don't tell me about my world. You're the one that's
afraid. You just want to have your little fling with the
guy from the other side of town and marry—

                    SKYLAR
Is that what you think—

WILL

—some prick from Stanford that your parents will approve of. Then you'll sit around with the rest of the upper-crust kids and talk about how you went slummin', too.

SKYLAR

I inherited that money when I was thirteen, when my father died.

WILL

At least you have a mother.

SKYLAR

Fuck you! You think I want this? That money's a burden to me. Every day I wake up and I wish I could give that back. I'd give everything I have back to spend one more day with my father. But that's life. And I deal with it. So don't put that shit on me. You're the one that's afraid.

WILL

What the fuck am I afraid of?!

SKYLAR

You're afraid of me. You're afraid that I won't love you back. And guess what? I'm afraid, too. But at least I have the balls to give it a shot. At least I'm honest with you.

WILL

I'm not honest?

SKYLAR

What, about your twelve brothers?

WILL

Oh, is that what this is about? You want to hear that I don't really have any brothers? That I'm a fuckin' orphan? Is that what you want to hear?

SKYLAR

Yes, Will. I didn't even know that.

                              WILL
No, you don't want to hear that.

                             SKYLAR
Yes, I do, Will.

                              WILL
You don't want to hear that I got cigarettes put out on
me when I was a little kid. That this isn't surgery—that
the motherfucker stabbed me.

Will lifts his shirt, revealing a six-inch SCAR on his torso.

                              WILL
You don't want to hear that. Don't tell me you want to
hear that shit!!

                             SKYLAR
Yes, I do. Did you ever think that maybe I could help
you? That maybe that's the point, that we're a team?

                              WILL
What, you want to come in here and save me? Is that
what you want to do? Do I have a sign that says "save
me" on my back?

                             SKYLAR
I don't want to save you. I just want to be with you. I
love you. I love you!

Will, full of self-loathing, raises his hand to strike her.

                              WILL
Don't bullshit me! Don't you fuckin' bullshit me!

                             SKYLAR
                      (standing up to him)
You know what I want to hear? I want to hear that
you don't love me. If you tell me that, then I'll leave
you alone. I won't ask any questions and I won't be in
your life.

A beat. Will looks Skylar dead in the eye. Lowers his hand.

WILL

I don't love you.

He walks out.

CUT TO:

■ **EXT. SKYLAR'S DORM—NIGHT**

Will leaves pulling on his clothes.

CUT TO:

■ **INT. NATIONAL SECURITY AGENCY, OFFICE—DAY**

Will sits across from two N.S.A. AGENTS, OLIVER DYTRESS and ROBERT TAVANO. These guys are smug, clean cut, gung ho, and looking sharp in twin navy blue suits.

WILL

So why do you think I should work for the National Security Agency?

DYTRESS

Well, you'd be working on the cutting edge. You'd be exposed to the kind of technology you couldn't see anywhere else because we've classified it. Superstring theory, chaos math, advanced algorithms—

WILL

Code breaking.

DYTRESS

That's one aspect of what we do.

WILL

Come on, that's what you do. You handle more than eighty percent of the intelligence workload. You're seven times the size of the C.I.A.

DYTRESS

That's exactly right, Will. So the question, as I see it, isn't "Why should you work for N.S.A.," it's "Why shouldn't you?"

WILL

Why shouldn't I work for the National Security Agency? That's a tough one.

Will bites his tongue, trying to make this work.

CUT TO:

■ INT. CHUCKIE'S HOUSE—DAY

Chuckie, Billy and Will sit in the Sullivan kitchen. Billy cracks open a beer and Chuckie reads the sports page. Both boys are smoking. Will drinks a beer distractedly. We hear the faint music track and soft moans of a PORNO MOVIE emanating from a back room. After a beat, Chuckie looks up.

CHUCKIE

Morgan, if you're watchin' pornos in my mom's room again I'm gonna give you a fuckin' beatin'!

After a beat, Morgan comes out of the back room, red-faced.

MORGAN
(innocently)

What's up guys?

CHUCKIE

Why don't you beat off at your house?

MORGAN

I don't have a VCR at my house.

Will pays no attention to this exchange.

CUT TO:

■ EXT. SOUTH BOSTON PAY PHONE—DAY

Will is on pay phone talking to Skylar.

> WILL
>
> I just wanted to call before you left.
>
> *(beat)*
>
> I'm takin' all these job interviews. So I won't just be a construction worker.

■ **INT. SKYLAR'S DORM—DAY**

> SKYLAR
>
> I never cared about that.

An awkward beat.

> WILL
>
> Yeah.

> SKYLAR
>
> I love you, Will.
>
> *(pause)*
>
> No take-backs.

Will says nothing.

> SKYLAR
>
> Will?

A beat.

> WILL
>
> Take care.

> SKYLAR
>
> Good-bye.

Will hangs up. Hold on him for an agonizing beat.

CUT TO:

■ **INT. SEAN'S OFFICE—DAY**

Lambeau is scribbling away at work. Tom is taking notes. Will is tapping his fingers, waiting for him to finish.

                         LAMBEAU
          I can . . . I'm almost there.

CUT TO:

■ **INT. LOGAN AIRPORT TERMINAL—SAME**

*Skylar stands at the gate, carry-ons in hand. Her flight is boarding. She looks
for Will over the crowd.*

CUT TO:

■ **INT. SEAN'S OFFICE—SAME**

*Will picks up a FRAME from Sean's desk. It is CARLTON FISK'S
BASEBALL CARD. Will has to smile. Lambeau looks up.*

                         LAMBEAU
          What are you smiling at?

                           WILL
          It's a Carleton Fisk baseball card.

Will can see that Lambeau wants more.

                           WILL
          Pudge Fisk. You follow baseball?

                         LAMBEAU
          No.

CUT TO:

■ **INT. LOGAN AIRPORT TERMINAL—SAME**

*The final boarding call is announced and the last passenger boards. After a beat,
Skylar turns and gets on the plane.*

CUT BACK TO:

■ **INT. SEAN'S OFFICE—SAME**

Will, holding the card, reflects for a beat and puts it down.

WILL

Oh, well, it's just somethin' Sean told me. It's a long story.
(*beat*)

You all set?

LAMBEAU

I've got the first part. The rest I can do at home.

Will gets up.

LAMBEAU

Will, the N.S.A. has been calling me just about every hour. They're very excited about how the meeting went.

Lambeau is excited. Will clearly is not.

                    WILL
  Yeah.

CUT TO:

■ INT. SEAN'S OFFICE—NIGHT

Will sits across from Sean.

                    SEAN
  So you might be working for Uncle Sam.

                    WILL
  I don't know.

                    SEAN
  Gerry says the meeting went well.

                    WILL
  I guess.

                    SEAN
  What did you think?

                    WILL
  What did I think?

A beat. Will has obviously been stewing on this.

                    WILL
  Say I'm working at N.S.A. Somebody puts a code on
  my desk, something nobody else can break. So I take a
  shot at it and maybe I break it. And I'm real happy
  with myself, 'cause I did my job well. But maybe that
  code was the location of some rebel army in North Af-
  rica or the Middle East. Once they have that location,
  they bomb the village where the rebels were hiding and
  fifteen hundred people I never had a problem with get
  killed.
                    (rapid fire)
  Now the politicians are sayin', "Send in the marines to
  secure the area" 'cause they don't give a shit. It won't
  be their kid over there, gettin' shot. Just like it wasn't

them when their number got called, 'cause they were
pullin' a tour in the National Guard. It'll be some guy
from Southie takin' shrapnel in the ass. And he comes
home to find that the plant he used to work at got ex-
ported to the country he just got back from. And the
guy who put the shrapnel in his ass got his old job,
'cause he'll work for fifteen cents a day and no bathroom breaks. Meanwhile my buddy from Southie realizes the only reason he was over there was so we could
install a government that would sell us oil at a good
price. And of course the oil companies used the skir-
mish to scare up oil prices so they could turn a quick
buck. A cute little ancillary benefit for them but it ain't
helping my buddy at two-fifty a gallon. And naturally
they're takin' their sweet time bringin' the oil back, and
maybe even took the liberty of hiring an alcoholic skip-
per who likes to drink martinis and play slalom with
the icebergs, and it ain't too long 'til he hits one, spills
the oil and kills all the sea life in the North Atlantic. So
my buddy's out of work and he can't afford to drive, so
he's got to walk to the job interviews, which sucks
'cause the shrapnel in his ass is givin' him chronic hem-
orrhoids. And meanwhile he's starvin' 'cause every time
he tries to get a bite to eat the only blue plate special
they're servin' is North Atlantic scrod with Quaker
State.

(beat)

So what'd I think? I'm holdin' out for somethin' better.
I figure I'll eliminate the middleman. Why not just
shoot my buddy, take his job and give it to his sworn
enemy, hike up gas prices, bomb a village, club a baby
seal, hit the hash pipe and join the National Guard?
Christ, I could be elected president.

                         SEAN
Do you think you're alone?

                         WILL
What?

                         SEAN
Do you have a soul mate?

                    WILL

Define that.

                    SEAN

Someone who challenges you in every way. Who takes
you places, opens things up for you. A soul mate.

                    WILL

Yeah.

Sean waits.

                    WILL

Shakespeare, Nietzsche, Frost, O'Connor, Chaucer,
Pope, Kant—

                    SEAN

They're all dead.

                    WILL

Not to me, they're not.

                    SEAN

But you can't give back to them, Will.

                    WILL

Not without a heater and some serious smelling salts,
no . . .

                    SEAN

That's what I'm saying, Will. You'll never have that
kind of relationship in a world where you're afraid to
take the first step because all you're seeing are the nega-
tive things that might happen ten miles down the road.

                    WILL

Oh, what? You're goin' to take the professor's side on
this?

                    SEAN

Don't give me your line of shit.

WILL

I didn't want the job.

SEAN

It's not about that job. I'm not saying you should work for the government. But you could do anything you want. And there are people who work their whole lives layin' brick so their kids have a chance at the kind of opportunity you have. What do you want to do?

WILL

I didn't ask for this.

SEAN

Nobody gets what they ask for, Will. That's a cop-out.

WILL

Why is it a cop-out? I don't see anythin' wrong with layin' brick. That's somebody's home I'm buildin'. Or fixin' somebody's car—somebody's gonna get to work the next day 'cause of me. There's honor in that.

SEAN

You're right, Will. Any man who takes a forty-minute train ride so those college kids can come in in the morning and their floors will be clean and their trash cans will be empty is an honorable man.

A beat. Will says nothing.

SEAN

And when they get drunk and puke in the sink, they don't have to see it the next morning because of you. That's real work, Will. And there is honor in that. Which I'm sure is why you took the job.
> *(beat)*

I just want to know why you decided to sneak around at night, writing on chalkboards and lying about it.
> *(beat)*

'Cause there's no honor in that.

Will is silent.

SEAN

Something you want to say?

Sean gets up, goes to the door and opens it.

SEAN

Why don't you come back when you have an answer
for me.

WILL

What?

SEAN

If you won't answer my questions, you're wasting my
time.

WILL

What?

Will loses it, slams the door shut.

WILL

Fuck you!

Sean has finally gotten to Will.

WILL

Who the fuck are you to lecture me about life? You
fuckin' burnout! Where's your "soul mate"?!

Sean lets this play out.

WILL

Dead! She dies and you just cash in your chips. That's a
fuckin' cop-out!

SEAN

I been there. I played my hand.

WILL

That's right. And you fuckin' lost! And some people
would have the sack to lose a big hand like that and still
come back and ante up again!

SEAN

Look at me. What do you want to do?

A beat. Will looks up.

SEAN

You and your bullshit. You got an answer for everybody. But I asked you a straight question and you can't
give me a straight answer. Because you don't know.

Sean goes to the door and opens it. Will walks out.

CUT TO:

■ **INT. MAGGIORE BUILDERS' CONSTRUCTION SITE—DAY**

*Will and Chuckie take crowbars to a wall. This is what they do for a living. As
they routinely hammer away, Will becomes more involved in his battle with the
wall. Plaster and lathing fly as Will vents his rage. Chuckie, noticing, stops
working and takes a step back, watching Will. Will is oblivious.*

CUT TO:

■ **INT. SEAN'S OFFICE—DAY**

*Lambeau and Tom are in his office. Will is nowhere to be seen. Lambeau is on
the phone.*

LAMBEAU

What I mean, Sean, is that I'm sitting in your office
and the boy isn't here.
                    (beat)
Well, it's ten past three.
                    (beat)
An *hour* and ten minutes late.
                    (beat)
Well, if he doesn't show up and I have to file a report
saying he wasn't here and he goes back to jail, it won't
be on my conscience, Sean.
                    (beat)
Fine.

He hangs up. Tom picks a FORM up off the desk.

                              TOM
What should I do?

                              LAMBEAU
The boy was here. He came in, sat down and we
worked together.

A blank look.

                              LAMBEAU
He came in, sat down and we worked together.

                              TOM
    Okay.

Tom understands, begins filling out the form.

CUT TO:

■ EXT. HANRAHAN'S PACKAGE STORE—LATER

Will walks out carrying a brown bag. He is filthy, having just knocked off work.

CUT TO:

■ EXT. MAGGIORE BUILDERS' CONSTRUCTION SITE—PARKING LOT

*Chuckie is sitting on the hood of his Cadillac, watching Will across the street.
Chuckie is covered in grime as well. Will starts walking toward Chuckie. As he
draws closer, he heaves a can of beer a good thirty yards to Chuckie, who handles
it routinely.*

*Will takes a seat next to Chuckie and they crack open their beers. Other workers
file out of the site. They drink.*

                              CHUCKIE
    How's the woman?

                              WILL
    Gone.

                              CHUCKIE
    What?

WILL

She went to medical school in California.

CHUCKIE

Sorry, brother.
(beat)
I don't know what to tell ya. You know all the girls I been with. You been with 'em too, except for Cheryl McGovern, which was a big mistake on your part, brother . . .

WILL

Oh, I'm sure, that's why only one of us has herpes.

CHUCKIE

Some shows are worth the price of admission, partner.

This gets a small laugh from Will.

CHUCKIE

My fuckin' back is killin' me.

A passing SHEET METAL WORKER overhears this.

SHEET METAL WORKER

That's why you shoulda gone to college.

WILL

Fuck you.

CHUCKIE

Suck my crank. Fuckin' sheet metal pussy.
(beat)
So, when are you done with those meetin's?

WILL

Week after I'm twenty-one.

CHUCKIE

Are they hookin' you up with a job?

WILL

Yeah, sit in a room and do long division for the next fifty years.

CHUCKIE

Yah, but it's better than this shit. At least you'd make some nice bank.

WILL

Yeah, be a fuckin' lab rat.

CHUCKIE

It's a way outta here.

WILL

What do I want a way outta here for? I want to live here for the rest of my life. I want to be your next-door neighbor. I want to take our kids to Little League together up Foley Field.

CHUCKIE

Look, you're my best friend, so don't take this the wrong way, but in twenty years, if you're livin' next

door to me, comin' over, watching the fuckin' Patriots'
game and still workin' construction, I'll fuckin' kill you.
And that's not a threat; that's a fact. I'll fuckin' kill you.

WILL

Chuckie, what are you talkin' . . .

CHUCKIE

Listen, you got somethin' that none of us have.

WILL

Why is it always this? I owe it to myself? What if I
don't want to?

CHUCKIE

Fuck you. You owe it to me. Tomorrow I'm gonna
wake up and I'll be fifty and I'll still be doin' this. And
that's all right 'cause I'm gonna make a run at it.
                    (beat)
But you, you're sittin' on a winning lottery ticket and
you're too much of a pussy to cash it in. And that's
bullshit 'cause I'd do anything to have what you got!
And so would any of these guys. It'd be a fuckin' insult
to us if you're still here in twenty years.

WILL

You don't know that.

CHUCKIE

Let me tell you what I do know. Every day I come by
to pick you up, and we go out drinkin' or whatever
and we have a few laughs. But you know what the best
part of my day is? The ten seconds before I knock on
the door, 'cause I let myself think I might get there,
and you'd be gone. I'd knock on the door and you
wouldn't be there. You just left.
                    (a beat)
Now, I don't know much. But I know that.

CUT TO:

■ **INT. SEAN'S OFFICE—DAY**

Lambeau stands across from Sean, seething.

> LAMBEAU
>
> This is a disaster! I brought you in here to help me
> with this boy, not to run him out—

> SEAN
>
> Now, wait a minute—

> LAMBEAU
>
> —and confuse him—

> SEAN
>
> Gerry—

> LAMBEAU
>
> —And here I am, for the second week in a row, with
> my professional reputation at stake—

> SEAN
>
> Hold on!

> LAMBEAU
>
> —ready to falsify documents because you've given him
> license to walk away from this.

> SEAN
>
> I know what I'm doing and I know why I'm here!

> LAMBEAU
>
> Look Sean, I don't care if you have a rapport with the
> boy—I don't care if you have a few laughs—even at
> my expense! But don't you dare undermine what I'm
> trying to do here.

> SEAN
>
> "Undermine?"

LAMBEAU

He has a gift, and with that gift comes responsibility.
And you don't understand that he's at a fragile point—

SEAN

He is at a fragile point. He's got problems—

LAMBEAU

What problems does he have, Sean, that he is better off
as a janitor or in jail or hanging around with—

SEAN

Why do you think he does that, Gerry?

LAMBEAU

He can handle the work, he can handle the pressure
and he's obviously handled you.

SEAN

Why is he hiding? Why is he a janitor? Why doesn't he
trust anybody? Because the first thing that happened to
him was that he was abandoned by the people who
were supposed to love him the most!

LAMBEAU

Oh, come on, Sean—

SEAN

And why does he hang out with his friends? Because
any one of those kids would come in here and take a
bat to your head if he asked them to. It's called loyalty!

LAMBEAU

Oh, that's nice—

SEAN

And who do you think he's handling? He pushes people away before they have a chance to leave him. And
for twenty years he's been alone because of that. And if
you try to push him into this, it's going to be the same
thing all over again. And I'm not going to let that happen to him!

LAMBEAU

Now don't do that. Don't you do that! Don't infect him with the idea that it's okay to quit. That's it okay to be a failure, because it's not okay! If you're angry at me for being successful, for being what you could have been—

SEAN

I'm not angry at you—

LAMBEAU

Yes, you are, Sean. You resent me. And I'm not going to apologize for any success that I've had.

SEAN

—I don't have any anger at you—

LAMBEAU

Yes you do. You're angry at me for doing what you could have done. Ask yourself if you want Will to feel that way for the rest of his life, to feel like a failure.

SEAN

That's it. That's why I don't come to the goddamn re-unions! Because I can't stand the look in your eye when you see me! You think I'm a failure! I know who I am. I'm proud of who I am. And all of you, you think I'm some kind of pity case!
(beat)
You with your sycophant students following you around. And your goddamn medal!

LAMBEAU

Is that what this is about, Sean? The Field's Medal? Do you want me to go home and get it for you? Then will you let the boy—

SEAN

—I don't want your trophy and I don't give a shit about it! 'Cause I knew you when!! You and Jack and Tom Sanders. I knew you when you were homesick

137

and pimply-faced and didn't know what side of the bed to piss on!

                    LAMBEAU

That's right! You were smarter than us then and you're smarter than us now! So don't blame me for how your life turned out. It's not my fault.

                    SEAN

I don't blame you! It's not about that! It's about the boy! 'Cause he's a good kid! And I won't see this happen to him—I won't see you make him feel like a failure too!

                    LAMBEAU

He won't be a failure!

                    SEAN

If you push him into something, if you ride him—

                    LAMBEAU

You're wrong, Sean. I'm where I am today because I was pushed. And because I learned to push myself!

                    SEAN

He's not you!

A beat. Lambeau turns, something catches his eye. Sean turns to look. IT'S WILL. He is standing in the doorway.

                    WILL

I can come back.

                    LAMBEAU

No, that's fine, Will. I was just leaving.

There is an awkward moment as Lambeau gets his coat and leaves.

                              WILL
Well, I'm here.
                              (beat)
So, is that my problem? I'm afraid of being abandoned?
That was easy.

                              SEAN
Look, a lot of that stuff goes back a long way. And it's
between me and him and it has nothing to do with
you.

                              WILL
Do you want to talk about it?

Sean smiles. A beat. Will sees a FILE on Sean's desk.

                              WILL
What's that?

                              SEAN
Oh, this is your file. I have to send it back to the judge
with my evaluation.

                              WILL
You're not gonna fail me are you?

Sean smiles.

                              WILL
So what's it say?

                              SEAN
You want to read it?

                              WILL
No.
                              (beat)
Have you had any experience with that?

                              SEAN
Twenty years of counseling, you see a lot of—

                              WILL
—No, have you had any experience with that?

                              SEAN
Yes.

                              WILL
                            (smiles)
It sure ain't good.

CUT TO:

■ **INT. WILL'S CHILDHOOD APARTMENT—FLASHBACK**

From a child's P.O.V. we see a man, partially obscured by a door frame. The man turns toward the P.O.V.

CUT BACK TO:

■ **INT. SEAN'S OFFICE—DAY**

                              SEAN
                         (after a pause)
My dad used to make us walk down to the park and
collect the sticks he was going to beat us with. Actually
the worst of the beatings were between me and my
brother. We would practice on each other, trying to
find sticks that would break.

                              WILL
He used to just put a belt, a stick and a wrench on the
kitchen table and say, "Choose."

CUT TO:

■ **INT. WILL'S CHILDHOOD APARTMENT—FLASHBACK**

A large, callused hand sets down a wrench next to a stick.

CUT BACK TO:

■ INT. SEAN'S OFFICE—DAY

SEAN
Gotta go with the belt, there. . . .

WILL
I used to go with the wrench.

SEAN
The wrench, why?

WILL
'Cause fuck him, that's why.

A long, quiet moment.

WILL
Is that why me and Skylar broke up?

SEAN
I didn't know you had. Do you want to talk about
that?
(*beat*)
I don't know a lot, Will. But let me tell you one thing.
All this history, this shit . . .
(*indicates file*)
Look here, son.

Will, who had been looking away, looks at Sean.

SEAN
This is not your fault.

WILL
(*nonchalant*)
Oh, I know.

SEAN
It's not your fault.

                         WILL
                         (smiles)
I know.

                         SEAN
It's not your fault.

                         WILL
I know.

                         SEAN
It's not your fault.

                         WILL
                         (dead serious)
I know.

                         SEAN
It's not your fault.

                         WILL
Don't fuck with me.

                         SEAN
              (comes around desk, sits in front of Will)
It's not your fault.

                         WILL
                         (tears start)
I know.

                         SEAN
It's not . . .

                         WILL
                         (crying hard)
I know, I know . . .

Sean takes Will in his arms and holds him like a child. Will sobs like a baby.
After a moment, he wraps his arms around Sean and holds him even tighter.
We pull back from this image. Two lonely souls being father and son together.

■ **INT. RED LINE CAR—DUSK**

Will rides the Red Line, above ground. He looks out over the landscape. Small backyards, with laundry hanging from wire lines. Chain-link fences overgrown with weeds.

■ **EXT. SOUTH BOSTON PARK—DAY**

Will walking through South Boston. He cuts through a park. A senior citizen is spearing trash for the city.

■ **INT. WILL'S APARTMENT—NIGHT**

Will at home. Not reading. Looks up at the ceiling.

■ **EXT. MCNEIL LABORATORIES—DAY**

Will walks up to a nondescript building, through the glass doors and into the lobby.

CUT TO:

■ **INT. MCNEIL LABORATORIES, RECEPTION—CONTINUOUS**

Will walks into the lobby. A SECURITY GUARD looks up.

> **SECURITY GUARD**
> Can I help you?

> **WILL**
> Yeah, my name is Will Hunting. I'm here about a position.

> **SECURITY GUARD**
> One moment.

The Guard reaches for the phone.
DISSOLVE TO BLACK.
FADE UP to the sound of laughter.

■ **INT. L STREET BAR & GRILLE—DAY**

Chuckie is again regaling Will and the guys at their table.

CHUCKIE

Oh my God, I got the most fucked-up thing I been meanin' to tell you.

MORGAN

Save it for your mother, funny guy. We heard it before.

CHUCKIE

Oh, Morgan.

They both get up, in each other's face. This is a play fight. "You gonna start?" "You gonna pay my hospital bills?"

WILL

Sorry to miss this.

■ INT. L STREET—SAME

Will comes back from the bathroom.

WILL
(to Chuckie)
You and Morgan throw?

CHUCKIE
No, I had to talk him down.

WILL
Why didn't you yoke him?

CHUCKIE
Little Morgan's got a lotta scrap, dude. I'd rather fight a big kid, they never fight, everyone's scared of 'em. You know how many people try to whip Morgan's ass every week? Fuckin' kid won't back down.

MORGAN
(from across the table)
What'd you say about me?

CHUCKIE
Shut the fuck up.

Billy walks in the door and gives Chuckie a look. Chuckie turns to Will.

CHUCKIE
(To Will)
Hey, asshole. Happy birthday.

MORGAN
You thought we forgot, didn't you? I know I'm gettin' my licks in.

Laughter as the boys converge on Will. He goes willingly out the door.

■ EXT. L STREET—CONTINUOUS

As they come out the door, rather than beating Will mercilessly, they stop. Morgan goes into his own, personal rendition of "Danny Boy." No one joins in.

CHUCKIE
Shut up, Morgan.

(to Will)

Here's your present.

Chuckie indicates an old CHEVY NOVA, parked illegally in front of the bar.

WILL

You're kiddin' me.

CHUCKIE

Yeah, I figured now that you got your big job over in
Cambridge, you needed some way to get over there
and I knew I wasn't gonna drive you every day. . . .

Laughter.

CHUCKIE

Morgan wanted to get you a T pass.

MORGAN

No I didn't. . . .

Will approaches the car to take a closer look.

CHUCKIE

But, you're twenty-one now, so—

BILLY

Yeah, now that you can drink legally, we thought the
best thing to get you was a car.

More laughter. Will inspects the Nova.

WILL
(beat)

You're kiddin' me.

This is the ugliest fuckin' car I ever seen in my life.

Laughter, a beat.

WILL
(serious)

How the fuck did you guys do this?

146

CHUCKIE

Me and Bill scraped together the parts, worked on it.
Morgan was out panhandlin' every day.

MORGAN

Fuck you, I did body work. Whose fuckin' router you
think sanded out all that rust?

CHUCKIE

Guy's been up my ass for two years about a fuckin' job.
I had to let him help with the car.

WILL

So, you finally got a job, Morgan?

MORGAN

Had one, now I'm fucked again.

WILL
(to Chuckie)
So what'd you do? Drop a fuckin' lawn-mower engine
in there? Will I make it back to my house?

CHUCKIE

Fuck you. I rebuilt the engine myself. That thing could make it to Hawaii if you wanted it to.

Chuckie gives Will a look.

CHUCKIE

Happy twenty-one, Will.

CUT TO:

■ **INT. SEAN'S OFFICE—DAY**

Will sits across from Sean.

SEAN

Which one did you take, Will?

WILL

Over at McNeil. One of the jobs Professor Lambeau set me up with. I haven't told him yet, but I talked to my new boss over there and he seemed like a nice guy.

SEAN

That's what you want?

WILL

Yeah, I think so.

SEAN

Good for you. Congratulations.

WILL

Thank you.
                    (beat)
So, that's it? We're done?

SEAN

We're done. You did your time. You're a free man.

A beat.

                    WILL
I just want you to know, Sean . . .

                    SEAN
You're welcome, Will.

                    WILL
I'll keep in touch.

                    SEAN
I'm gonna travel a little bit, so I don't know where I'll
be.

Will smiles.

                    SEAN
I just . . . figured it's time I put my money back on the
table, see what kind of cards I get.

Will smiles. Sean hands him a piece of paper.

                    SEAN
I'll be checking in with my machine at the college. If
you ever need anything, just call.

Sean smiles.

                    SEAN
Do what's in your heart, son. You'll be fine.

                    WILL
Thank you, Sean.

They embrace.

                    SEAN
No. Thank you.

                    WILL
                (re-embrace)
Does this violate the patient/doctor relationship?

                              SEAN
          Only if you grab my ass.

They laugh.

                              WILL
          See ya.

                              SEAN
          Good luck.

Both men smile.

CUT TO:

■ **INT. HALLWAY OUTSIDE SEAN'S OFFICE—MOMENTS LATER**

Will comes out of Sean's office and sees Lambeau walking up.

                            LAMBEAU
                            (surprised)
          Will.

                              WILL
          Hey, how you doin'?

                            LAMBEAU
          You know, you're no longer required to come here.

                              WILL
          I was just sayin' good-bye to Sean.

                            LAMBEAU
                              (beat)
          Sam called me. From McNeil. He says you start work-
          ing for them next week.

Will nods.

                            LAMBEAU
          Well, that's . . . I think that's terrific. Congratulations.

                              WILL
Thank you.

                           LAMBEAU
I just want you to know . . . It's been a pleasure.

                              WILL
Bullshit.

They laugh.

                           LAMBEAU
This job . . . Do it if it's what you really want.

                              WILL
I appreciate that.

*A moment. Will starts to go, Lambeau watches him for a beat, Will turns back
around.*

                              WILL
Hey, Gerry.

                           LAMBEAU
Yes?

                              WILL
Listen, I'll be nearby, so if you need some help, or you
get stuck again, don't be afraid to give me a call.

                           LAMBEAU
                         (has to smile)
Thank you, Will. I'll do that.

Will smiles, turns and walks away.

■ **INT. SEAN'S OFFICE—DAY**

Sean is packing his office. Lambeau opens the door.

                           LAMBEAU
Hello, Sean.

                    SEAN
Come in.

                    LAMBEAU
Sean . . .

                    SEAN
                    (beat)
Me, too.

A moment.

                    LAMBEAU
So I hear you're taking some time.

                    SEAN
Yeah. Summer vacation. Thought I'd travel some.
Maybe write a little bit.

                    LAMBEAU
Where're you going?

                    SEAN
I don't know. India maybe.

                    LAMBEAU
Why there?

                    SEAN
Never been.

Lambeau nods.

                    LAMBEAU
Do you know when you'll be back?

                    SEAN
Well,
          (picks up a flyer from his desk)
I got this mailer the other day. Class of 'seventy-two is
having this event in six months.

                              LAMBEAU
I got one of those, too.

                               SEAN
You should come. I'll buy you a drink.

Lambeau smiles.

                              LAMBEAU
Sean . . .
                              (beat)
The drinks at those things are free.

Sean smiles.

                               SEAN
Hell, I know that.

Both men laugh.

                              LAMBEAU
How about one now?

                               SEAN
Sounds good.

They start to walk out.

                               SEAN
It's on you, though, until eight o'clock tonight when I
win my money.

Sean pulls out his lottery ticket. They start out down the hall.

CUT TO:

■ INT. HALLWAY—CONTINUOUS

On their backs as they walk down the hall.

                              LAMBEAU
Sean, do you have any idea what the odds are against
winning the lottery?

SEAN

I don't know . . . Gotta be at least four to one.

LAMBEAU

About thirty million to one.

SEAN

You're pretty quick with those numbers. How about
the odds of me buying the first round?

LAMBEAU

About thirty million to one.

CUT TO:

■ EXT. BANK OF THE CHARLES RIVER—AFTERNOON

*Will sits alone, thinking. We hold on him for an extended beat until he gets up
and walks away.*

■ EXT. SEAN'S APARTMENT—EARLY EVENING

Begin final sequence.

*A wide, establishing shot of Sean's apartment complex as the sun is setting. The
lights are on in one unit. A tighter shot reveals Sean, in his apartment, packing
his belongings in cardboard boxes.*

■ EXT. SEAN'S APARTMENT, STREET—SAME

*The camera cranes down from Sean's window and onto the street, where we pan
to reveal Will, sitting in his car and looking up at Sean as he packs his things.
Will's car is packed full of clothes and books.*

■ EXT. SOUTH BOSTON STREET—SAME

*Chuckie and the boys drive down the street in the Cadillac. Morgan and Billy
ride in the back, leaving the shotgun seat open for Will.*

■ EXT. SEAN'S APARTMENT—SAME

Will holds an envelope which he slips into Sean's mailbox. He puts the flag up and smiles as he looks up at Sean, in his apartment and still unaware that Will is there.

■ EXT. WILL'S APARTMENT—SAME

Chuckie pulls up in front of Will's house. He honks the horn, waits a beat, then gets out and heads toward the house.

■ EXT. SEAN'S APARTMENT—SAME

Will drives away from Sean's house. Sean hears the car pull out and looks out the window. Sean sees Will's car pulling away. Curious, he investigates.

■ EXT. WILL'S APARTMENT—SAME

Chuckie walks up Will's front steps.

■ EXT. SEAN'S APARTMENT—SAME

Sean walks out to the sidewalk and looks around. Seeing that the mailbox flag has been raised, he walks over to it.

■ EXT. WILL'S APARTMENT—SAME

Chuckie knocks on Will's front door. There is no answer. He waits a beat, looks in the window. An incredulous smile slowly starts to form.

■ EXT. SEAN'S APARTMENT—SAME

Sean opens the card Will left for him. It reads:

> WILL
> *(in writing)*
> Sean—If the professor calls about that job, just tell him,
> "Sorry, I had to go see about a girl."

■ EXT. WILL'S APARTMENT—SAME

Chuckie walks back toward his car, unable to contain a broad smile. He knows Will is gone. He shrugs in explanation to the guys. Morgan takes Will's seat as they pull away from the curb.

■ EXT. SEAN'S APARTMENT—SAME

We pan up from the letter to Sean. A broad smile comes over him. This is a look we haven't seen. Sean is truly happy.

■ EXT. MASSACHUSETTS TURNPIKE—SUNSET

Will is on the road, driving away. As we pull back and credits roll, the car disappears into the horizon.

THE END

MIRAMAX FILMS
Presents

A LAWRENCE BENDER
Production

A Film by
GUS VAN SANT

ROBIN WILLIAMS

MATT DAMON

GOOD WILL HUNTING

BEN AFFLECK

STELLAN SKARSGÅRD

and MINNIE DRIVER

CASEY AFFLECK
COLE HAUSER

Casting by
BILLY HOPKINS
SUZANNE SMITH
KERRY BARDEN

Costume Designer
BEATRIX ARUNA PASZTOR

Music Supervisor
JEFFREY KIMBALL

Music By
DANNY ELFMAN

Editor
PIETRO SCALIA

Production Designer
MELISSA STEWART

Director of Photography
JEAN YVES ESCOFFIER

Co-Produced by
CHRIS MOORE

Co-Executive Producers
KEVIN SMITH
SCOTT MOSIER

Executive Producers
BOB WEINSTEIN
HARVEY WEINSTEIN
JONATHAN GORDON

Executive Producer
SU ARMSTRONG

Produced by
LAWRENCE BENDER

Written by
MATT DAMON
and
BEN AFFLECK

Directed by
GUS VAN SANT

(cast in order of appearance)

Will	MATT DAMON
Chuckie	BEN AFFLECK
Lambeau	STELLAN SKARSGÅRD
Tom	JOHN MIGHTON

Krystyn	RACHEL MAJOROWSKI
Cathy	COLLEEN McCAULEY
Morgan	CASEY AFFLECK
Billy	COLE HAUSER
Barbershop Quartet #1	MATT MERCIER
Barbershop Quartet #2	RALPH ST. GEORGE
Barbershop Quartet #3	ROB LYNDS
Barbershop Quartet #4	DAN WASHINGTON
M.I.T. Students	ALISON FOLLAND
	DERRICK BRIDGEMAN
	VIC SAHAY
Girl on Street	SHANNON EGLESON
Carmine Scarpaglia	ROB LYONS
Carmine Friend #1	STEVEN KOZLOWSKI
Skylar	MINNIE DRIVER
Lydia	JENNIFER DEATHE
Clark	SCOTT WILLIAM WINTERS
Head Custodian	PHILIP WILLIAMS
Assistant Custodian	PATRICK O'DONNELL
Courtroom Guard	KEVIN RUSHTON
Judge Malone	JIMMY FLYNN
Prosecutor	JOE CANNON
Court Officer	ANN MATACUNAS
Psychologist	GEORGE PLIMPTON
Hypnotist	FRANCESCO CLEMENTE
Sean	ROBIN WILLIAMS
Bunker Hill College Students	JESSICA MORTON
	BARNA MORICZ
Toy Store Cashier	LIBBY GELLER
M.I.T. Professor	CHAS LAWTHER
Bartender	RICHARD FITZPATRICK
Bar Patron	PATRICK O'DONNELL
Executive #1	FRANK NAKASHIMA
Executive #2	CHRIS BRITTON
Executive #3	DAVID EISNER
NSA Agent	BRUCE HUNTER
Security Guard	JAMES ALLODI
Stunt Coordinator	JERY HEWITT
Utility Stunt	BRIAN RICCI
Unit Production Manager	BRENT O'CONNOR
Unit Production Manager (Boston)	CHRISTOPHER GOODE
First Assistant Director	ANDREW SHEA

Second Assistant Director	DAVID TILL
Second Assistant Director (Boston)	LISA JANOWSKI
2nd 2nd Assistant Director (Boston)	BRIAN YORK
Title Design	PABLO FERRO
Post-Production Supervisors	BOB HACKL
	PAM WINN BARNETT
Post-Production Consultant	HEIDI VOGEL
Art Director	JAMES McATEER
1st Assistant Art Directors	MICHAEL MADDEN
	GORDON LeBREDT
2nd Assistant Art Director	MARK DUFFIELD
Set Decorator	JARO DICK
Production Coordinator	VAIR MACPHEE
Co-Production Coordinator	RANDY KUMANO
Travel Coordinator	SOPHIA LOFTERS
Production Accountant	APRIL JANOW
First Assistant Accountant	KILEY FASCIA
Accounting Clerk	SARAH THORNTON
Payroll Clerk	SUSAN REID
Script Supervisor	KATHRYN BUCK
Unit Location Manager	MARTY DEJCZAK
Assistant Location Manager	MARK LOGAN
1st Assistant Camera	RICK PEROTTO
2nd Assistant Camera	JOE MICOMONACO
Camera Trainee	PETER SWEENEY
Sound Mixer	OWEN LANGEVIN
Right Boom Operator	JIM THOMPSON
Left Boom Operator	ERICA SCHENGELI-ROBERTS
Dialect Coach	ROBERT EASTON
Jail Consultant	HARMONY KORINE
Math Consultant	PATRICK O'DONNELL
Psychology Consultant	DR. JOHN TURTLE
Make-up Artist	LESLIE SEBERT
Hairstylist	JAMES D. BROWN
Wardrobe Supervisor	DELPHINE WHITE
Set Costumers	GERRI GILLIAN
	MARCIA SCOTT
Assistant Costume Designer	VANESSA VOGEL

Gaffer	BRYAN FORDE
Best Boy Electric	DAVE KELLNER
Rigging Gaffer	HERB REISCHL
Electrics	ROBERT HANNAH
	WILLIAM McKIBBIN
	JAMES MacCAMMON
	KENNETH WYKE
	NEIL GOVER
Key Grip	MARK MANCHESTER
Best Boy Grip	MALCOLM NEFSKY
Dolly Grip	TRACY SHAW
Grips	JAMES KOHNE
	MATTHEW PILL
	WAYNE GOODCHILD
	STEVE KLYS
	BOB O'CONNOR
Assistant Decorator	JOHN "BUTCH" ROSE
On Set Dresser	DAVID CHARLES
Set Decorator Buyer	DANIELLE FLEURY
Property Master	MARC CORRIVEAU
Assistant Property Master	DAVID EVANS
Props Buyer	GRAEME "GOOSE" GOSSAGE
Greensman	MICHAEL ALLEGRETTO
Key Scenic Artist	REET PUHM
Head Painter	KIRK COPELLA
Construction Coordinator	PHIL TELLEZ
Construction Foreman	DUNCAN CAMPBELL
Location Head Carpenter	MARK O'DONOGHUE
Assistant Head Stand-By Carpenter	VITO BOTTICELLA
Welder	ALEX TELLNOW
First Assistant Editors	CHISAKO YOKOYAMA
	KELLEY C. DIXON
Assistant Editors	D-J
	KIM ROSEBOROUGH
Editing Intern	SCOTT PATRICK GREEN
Supervising Sound Editor	KELLEY BAKER
Re-Recording Mixers	LESLIE SHATZ, C.S.T.
	TOM DAHL
	GUS VAN SANT
Music Editor	KEN KARMAN

ADR/Walla Editor	PETER APPLETON
Dialogue Editor	DAVID A. COHEN
Sound Editors	MICHAEL GANDSEY "GONZO"
	RICHARD MOORE
	PATRICK WINTERS
Assistant Sound Editors	CONCHA SOLANO
	AARON OLSON
Assistant Music Editor	STEPHANIE LOWRY
Foley Artists	MARGIE O'MALLEY
	JENNIFER MYERS
	MARNIE MOORE
Foley Mixer	STEVE FONTANO
Foley Recordist	FRANK RINELLA
Post-Production Coordinator	JOLIE GORCHOV
Post-Production Accountant	DOUG BENSON
Executive for A Band Apart	COURTNEY McDONNELL
Unit Publicist	PRUDENCE EMERY
Still Photographer	GEORGE KRAYCHYK
Casting Director—Toronto	TINA GERUSSI
Extras Casting—Toronto	JANE ROGERS
Casting Assistant—New York	MARK BENNETT
Stand-In for Mr. Williams	ADAM BRYANT
Stand-Ins for Mr. Damon	ALEX ROSS
	EVANN TENOR
	BILL McADAMS
Stand-Ins for Mr. Ben Affleck	DEREK MILOSAVLJERIC
	DAVID MARSHALL
Stand-Ins for Ms. Driver	KRISTINA MEURING
	LAURIE LAPIDES
Stand-In for Mr. Skarsgård	JUSTIN BILL
Stand-Ins for Mr. Casey Affleck	IAN CAMPBELL
	MICHAEL McGROARTY
Stand-Ins for Mr. Hauser	P. ROBERT HUGHES
	ROBERT HOEHN
Assistant to Mr. Bender	JEFF SWAFFORD
Assistant to Ms. Armstrong	AMANDA WHITE
Assistant to Mr. Van Sant	SCOTT PATRICK GREEN
Assistant to Mr. Williams	REBECCA IRWIN SPENCER
Assistant to Mr. Damon & Mr. Affleck	DREW CLARKE
Assistant to Mr. Gordon	MICHELLE SY
A Band Apart Legal	CARLOS GOODMAN, JAMES KERSHAW, ANN DUVAL
	LICHTER, GROSSMAN, NICHOLS & ADLER, INC.

Music Legal Services	ERIC GREENSPAN
Miramax Legal	NEIL SACKER
	BRIAN BURKIN
Legal Immigration	MICHAEL ROSENFELD
3rd Assistant Director	JENNIFER DEATHE
DGC Trainee	KATE WEISS
Locations P.A.	DAVID McILLROY
Production Assistant	GORDON WEISKE
Office Production Assistants	CATHERINE SAMPLE
	BOB GLOVER
	CRAIG GOODWILL
Transportation Coordinator	DAVE STAPLES
Transportation Captain	STUART MITCHELL
Lead Driver	KEN BARBET
Drivers	GEORGE BAXTER
	PAT BRENNAN
	PERCY BUDD
	GARY FLANAGAN
	RAY GABOURIE
	STUART HUGHES
	GORDON JONSON
	NEIL MONTGOMERIE
	GREG O'HARA
	MAURICE TREMBLAY
Set Decorator Driver	RICARDO BURKHARDT
Toronto Catering	BY DAVID'S
Toronto Craft Service	STARCRAFT SERVICE, INC.
Special Effects	KAVANAUGH SPECIAL EFFECTS
Group ADR Coordinator	BERTON SHARP
Negative Cutter	GARY BURRITT
Color Timer	MICHAEL MERTENS

Boston Unit

Production Supervisor	DOROTHY AUFIERO
Production Coordinators	MARIANNE CRESCENZI
New York Production Coordinator	ROGER DAVIES
Production Secretary	MEG MONTAGNINO
First Assistant Accountant	BILL PHILLIPS
Accounting Clerk	DAVID RICCARDI
Unit Location Manager	CHARLES HARRINGTON

Assistant Location Manager	MARK FITZGERALD
Camera Operator	BRIAN HELLER
2nd Assistant Camera	ADAM GILMORE
Camera Loader	STEPHANIE RYAN
Center Boom Recordist	JAMES MASE
Additional Makeup Artist	JEAN CARNEY
Additional Hair Stylist	ELIZABETH CECCHINI
Wardrobe Supervisor	DEBBIE HOLBROOK
Set Costumers	DAWN TESTA
	ANN POWDERLY
	SUSAN ANDERSON
Wardrobe Dyer	LISA LESNIAK
Wardrobe P.A.	NANCY DRINAN
Best Boy Electric	SCOTT DAVIS
Electrics	MARK J. CASEY
	STEVE GIROUARD
	JACK MacPHEE
Best Boy Grip	THOMAS DORAN
Dolly Grip	ROBERT TOMPKINS
Grips	MARTIN ALBERT
	TIM DRISCOLL
	TIM HOGAN
Art Director	KENNETH A. HARDY
Set Decorator	KATHLEEN ROSEN
Leadman	PAUL RICHARDS
Second Man	KENNY DOYLE
On Set Dresser	PETER E. NAUYOKAS
Set Decorator Buyers	AILEEN SOVRONSKY
Set Dressers	MANYA CETLIN
	CHRIS "CURTIS" FOUSEK
	DONALD WILSON JR.
	STEVEN MORELL
Art Department Coordinator	LISA NAGID
Art Department P.A.	JESSICA CHAFFIN
Assistant Property Master	KRISTINE MORAN
Props Assistant	JENNIFER ENGEL
Set Designer	ADAM SCHER
Construction Coordinator	KURT SMITH
Construction Foreman	JUDSON BELL
Charge Scenic	DIANE LAURIENZO
Scenic Artists	ERIC LEVENSON
	KAREN MENZE
	VANESSA MILLS
	MARK TUCKER

On Set Scenic	CHRISTINE KASETA-CORNELIUS
Carpenters	EUGENE POPE
	JACK COYLE
Local Casting	CAROLYN PICKMAN C.S.A.
Extras Casting	COLLINGE/PICKMAN CASTING, INC.
	KEVIN FENNESSY
Extras Casting Assistant	MATTHEW BOULDRY
Locations P.A.	LUCIUS RAMSEY
Production Assistants	COLIN MacLELLAN
	TED ALVAREZ
	MARY DONOVAN
	JOHN LOUGHLIN
	LIZ O'KELLY
	AARON STOCKARD
	CHRISTIAN HOLLYER
Transportation Coordinator	BILLY O'BRIEN
Transportation Captain	BOBBY MARTINI
Drivers	NORMAN MAHONEY
	JOE GAGLIARDI
	ROBERT ALBANO
	BARTLEY SMALL
	CHARLIE HASKINS
	TOM COSTLEY
	ROBERT DESTASIO
	ROBERT DUDLEY
	WILLIAM McGRATE
	RICHARD HANSCOM
	JOE WARREN
	RON DUNDER
	GEORGE RUSSELL JR.
	JOSEPH F. RYAN JR.
	RICHARD ABATE JR.
	JAMES O'LEARY
	RICHARD BUTTARO
Cook Driver	CHRIS WARREN
Catering Assistants	MARTY IGNATOWSKI
	LARRY BABITZ
Craft Service	FRANK FOLEY
Special Effects Coordinator	BRIAN RICCI
SPFX	ED RICCI
	STEPHEN RICCI
	WILLIAM "BILLYJACK" JAKIELASZEK

Score Produced by   DANNY ELFMAN
Music Scoring Mixer   DENNIS SANDS
Music Clearances   JILL MEYERS

Soundtrack available on Capital CD's and cassettes

PHOTO: "DALI ATOMICUS" BY PHILIPPE HALSMAN
© HALSMAN ESTATE
MAJOR LEAGUE BASEBALL FOOTAGE PROVIDED COURTESY OF
MAJOR LEAGUE BASEBALL PRODUCTIONS. COPYRIGHT ©
MAJOR LEAGUE BASEBALL PROPERTIES, INC.
ALL RIGHTS RESERVED.
JOHN KIRBY PRINT COURTESY OF FLOWERS EAST, LONDON
HENRY MOORE LITHOGRAPHS © THE HENRY MOORE
FOUNDATION
REPRODUCED BY PERMISSION OF THE HENRY MOORE
FOUNDATION
DORIS McCARTHY WORK ENTITLED "GLACIER BAY"
COURTESY OF THE ARTIST
SAMUEL BECKETT PHOTOGRAPH COURTESY OF *THE IRISH
TIMES* LIMITED
VASARELY SERIOGRAPHS © 1997 ARTIST'S RIGHTS SOCIETY
(ARS), NEW YORK/ADAGP, PARIS
BOSTON HERALD APPEARS WITH PERMISSION OF *THE BOSTON
HERALD*
APPROACHES TO PSYCHOLOGY TEXT COURTESY OF WILLIAM E.
GLASSMAN
ALL TRADEMARKS AND COPYRIGHTS OF THE NATIONAL
HOCKEY LEAGUE AND ITS MEMBER TEAMS ARE USED WITH
PERMISSION. ALL RIGHTS RESERVED.

THE FILMMAKERS WISH TO THANK:

JULIE KIRKHAM	GERRY SPECA
NICOLE PENNINGTON	JACK McNEES
JOHN L. BURNHAM	JAY LACOPO
GABY MORGERMAN	KIM GREEN
LEE STOLLMAN	RICHARD FRANCIS
MIKE SIMPSON	JOHN HADITY
MICHAEL MENCHEL	KEVIN HYMAN
PATRICK WHITESELL	JACK LECHNER
DAVID RICCARDI	MERYL POSTER
DAVID WHEELER	AMY SLOTNICK
DERRICK BRIDGEMAN	JENNO TOPPING
ED ZWICK	ANDREW CANNAVA

ANTHONY KUBIAK
BOBBY CURCURO
CHEYENNE ROTHMAN
CHRIS MURPHY
CHUCK SAUCIER
JIMMY DARMODY
LIZ GLOTZER
MARK TUSK
MIKE NYLON
PAUL WEBSTER

PETER GARRISON
PETER YATES
RICHARD LINKLATER
ROB REINER
SAM FISHER
SKYLAR SATENSTEIN
STEVE BURKOW
TERRENCE MALICK
WILLIAM GOLDMAN

ONTARIO FILM DEVELOPMENT OFFICE—GAIL THOMPSON,
DONNA ZUCHLINSKY
TORONTO FILM OFFICE—DAVID PLANT
MASSACHUSETTS FILM OFFICE—ROBIN DAWSON—DIRECTOR,
TIM GRAFFT—DEPUTY DIRECTOR
THE STATE OF MASSACHUSETTS
THE CITY OF BOSTON
THE IRISH TIMES LIMITED
MERCHANTS AND RESIDENTS OF SOUTH BOSTON
BARBARA AND STEPHEN KOPLIN, ATLAS BISCUIT COMPANY
HEATHER REM AND ANN MARIE WILLIAMS AND REEBOK
ENTERTAINMENT
LARRY CANACRO AND THE BOSTON RED SOX
CAMBRIDGE RINDGE AND LATIN
THE PILOT SCHOOL

MATT DAMON AND BEN AFFLECK THANK THEIR FAMILY AND
FRIENDS

Wescam provided by	WESCAM USA, INC.
Wescam Operator	DAVID NORRIS
Wescam Technician	GREG HILL
Grip and Electric Equipment provided by	PANAVISION, TORONTO
Boston Catering provided by	DELUXE CATERING
Re-Recorded by	BUENA VISTA SOUND
Titles by	THE TITLE HOUSE
Opticals by	PACIFIC TITLE
Digital Opticals by	CINEMA RESEARCH CORPORATION

Travel Services Provided by	Javier Arqueros/TRAVELCORPS
Payroll Services Provided by	AXIUM PAYROLL SERVICES
Insurance provided by	AON/RUBEN-WINKLER GREAT NORTHERN BROKERAGE CORPORATION
Filmed in	PANAVISION
Photographed on	KODAK FILM
Dailies by	deluxe toronto
COLOR by	CFI

RECORDED IN DOLBY DIGITAL IN SELECTED THEATERS

MPAA# 35614
MOTION PICTURE ASSOCIATION OF AMERICA

In Memory of

Allen Ginsberg
&
William S. Burroughs